ON GETTING OLD
for the
FIRST TIME

ON GETTING OLD

for the

FIRST TIME

by

Emily

and

Peg Bracken

With verse and decorations by the author

 **BookPartners, Inc.**
Wilsonville, Oregon

OTHER BOOKS BY PEG BRACKEN

The 9-Months' Wonder (with Helen Berry Moore)
The I Hate to Cook Book
The I Hate to Housekeep Book
I Try to Behave Myself
Appendix to The I Hate to Cook Book
I Didn't Come Here to Argue
But I Wouldn't Have Missed It for the World!
The I Hate to Cook Almanack
The Compleat I Hate To Cook Book
A Window Over the Sink

Copyright 1997 by Peg Bracken
Second Printing
All rights reserved
Printed in U.S.A.
Cover cartoon by Deena Printz
Cover design by Richard Ferguson
Library of Congress Catalog 96-85316
ISBN 1-885221-53-3

BookPartners, Inc.
P.O. Box 922
Wilsonville, Oregon 97070

*For John Ohman
with my love.*

Table of Contents

Explanatory Note

I was talking with my editor, and he asked me how I happened to write this book.

"Well, I went to see the doctor recently," I said, "to complain about a sort of stiffness in my legs. And so he looked me over and didn't find anything really wrong, and then he said, 'Of course, you've never been this age before.'" (At the time, I was a mere child of 73.)

̅

And, of course, I hadn't. The doctor was right, I told my editor; I just didn't know it would feel like this. So the doctor told me to walk a lot and drink a glass of skim milk every day, and that was about it.

But on the way home, I wondered what other surprises were waiting for me as time jogged along. Was it Oliver Wendell Holmes or Charles Evans Hughes (I tend to confuse them, like the windward side and the lee side) who said that being old was like you

have soap in your ears and vaseline on your glasses and
rocks in your shoes…? I hadn't really noticed the soap
in my ears yet, and it wasn't vaseline on my glasses
exactly, more like a bit of olive oil from a pizza I might
have had for lunch. There were still no rocks in my
shoes, just tiny French peas.

ॐ

    "But who is Emily?" the editor asked.
    I tried to think, which isn't always easy.
    "Well…" I said uncertainly, thinking back, which
is even harder. "She appeared one day on the back of a
grocery list. I was doodling while trying to decide
between asparagus and green beans for dinner, and
suddenly there was Emily. I can't draw, which should
be obvious, and so she surprised me. When I doodle,
it's usually five-pointed stars — little ones, big ones, all
sizes, like this —

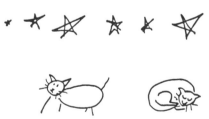

or cats —

but not people. I still don't. I just draw Emily."
    "And did Emily do the…er…verses?" the editor
asked.
    "No, she translated them, I believe," I explained.
"From the little-known works of Hu Shih."

"Who she?" the editor asked.

"That's right," I said. "Hu Shih was court poet [and, it's been rumored, concubine] to Hu Hih, emperor of China, some time during the Ming Dynasty. Of course, that was a long time ago, but it is amazing how relevant her work is to the modern age."

"Hmmmmm," the editor said. "Would you say she is perhaps your alter ego?"

"I just don't know," I said.

"Hmmmmm," the editor said.

Chapter One

Moving Right Along

Don't know where we'll end but hey,
Nevertheless we're on our way!

It is a shame that most things you do must be done for the first time, at least once. If only you could start with the second or third time, after you'd had some experience, you could probably do a better job.

This is true of very small things, like separating the egg white from the egg yolk, or filling your own gas tank, or applying false eyelashes. It is equally true of the large things, like getting born or married or having a baby, or — especially — getting Old. And there is certainly a lot of that going around, for it is a reasonably democratic process. If you are lucky, you get Old, and if you're not, you don't.

Not that it is a piece of cake. Getting Old is interesting country, as I am discovering. But it does present problems, one of the biggest being that in the present day and age you're not supposed to. Get Old, I mean.

You are reminded of the fact a dozen times daily by ads and commercials showing you how you should look and behave,[1] like the farmer putting the ostrich egg in the henhouse under a sign, *Look at This and Do Your Best.* But then the commercials get down to the nitty-gritty, especially in the late-afternoon newscasts,

---

1. The way teenagers do.

between five and eight. That is when they bring on the hemorrhoids and the heartburn, the loose dentures and the dragon breath, the bad backs and constipation that advertisers seem to think are the distinguishing marks of the chronologically challenged.

Queasy's the word for the audience, during Commercials that cause what they ought to be curing.

I'd like to know, where are the pimple creams? Where are the hair-styling mousses, the windsurfers' outdoor gear? Don't the young ever watch the early-evening news? Apparently not. The advertisers think their audience is composed entirely of frazzled old creeps who can hardly make it to the bathroom in time. But not to worry, our sponsors have extra-absorbent solutions for that too.

It's too bad, because it helps give getting Old a worse name than it deserves. Had there been television when I was young, I think I would have said, "Hand me the house pistol; I'm outa here." But I'm glad I didn't.

Still, it isn't surprising that you begin to feel — well, guilty isn't quite the word. *Abashed* is more like it. As though you'd been caught picking your teeth in public, or double-parking where you shouldn't. This can lead to coyness about admitting your age, and remarks like, *Oops, I'm dating myself!* should you happen to mention the great time you had at the New York World's Fair.

I suppose there has always been consider-able hypocrisy about getting Old or being Old. Way back in 1604, asserting the beauties of age, John Webster wrote:

"...*is not old wine wholesomest, old pippins toothsomest? Does not old wood burn brightest, old linen wash whitest? Old soldiers, sweethearts are surest, and old lovers are soundest....*"

Old age beautiful? Tell me what's
So fetching about liver spots

But let's (as we say now) get real. The answer is No, and this is the sort of nincompoopery one must beware of. Wine, after a certain point, becomes musty and sour. Old wood doesn't burn half so brightly as one of the new Magic Logs, which produce gorgeous salmon-and-purple flames (and if the old wood is the slightest bit damp, it won't burn at all). An old soldier is usually a broken record of tattered war stories, and when you see an old sweetheart or lover, you generally wonder, *what was the matter with my head?*

It seems clear that the basic premise here is suspect. People don't have to be told that ice cream tastes good; they'll figure that out for themselves. It is the Brussels sprouts that need the hard sell. And I think this is another thing that gives old age its bad name — this beaming emphasis on the positive at the occasional sacrifice of (forgive me for saying this) — the truth.

With few exceptions, people don't get substantially better-looking as they get older. The only ones I can think of are the Old couple that inhabits Channel 8. I think of them as the Silver-haired Cruise Couple, standing at the ship's rail against a rosy sunset. They have apparently overcome those personal digestive and dental problems mentioned earlier. Romantic as teenagers, they are usually holding hands when they are not toasting each other in a milky sort of drink that contains all known vitamins and minerals, and they certainly do travel a lot.

I don't know any other Old couple that looks quite like that except for the Silver-haired Fun Couple on Channel 6. They are always racing around in a convertible, hair blowing in the wind (they still have some), stopping only long enough to knock back a canful of another milky-looking liquid, probably sweetened with a dollop of gin, they look that happy.

It is impossible to tell, of course, just how much professional help they've had in maintaining these classy façades. But it's safe to bet they've had some, including the softest focus lens in the studio.

જ

Flying to Phoenix recently, as I was making notes about this book, a friendly young flight attendant asked if I were keeping a diary. I said "No," and told him I was writing a book about getting Old.

Refilling my coffee cup, he looked thoughtful. "You know, I've never really worried about that," he said. "I doubt if it's any worse than flying in light turbulence."

He didn't know that the turbulence can become a bit more turbulent as the years go by. All the same, I thought, that says it pretty well. As pilot, you have some interesting problems, keeping your speed up and your craft level (but whenever didn't you?) And if a wing falls off or you lost altitude or something, a certain confusion can set in. (*"Watch what you're* <u>*doing!*</u>*" I said to myself crossly as I put the ice cream away in the oven.*) However, I still think I'd choose growing Old anytime over growing up.

జ

And so I've been observing other people lately, as well as myself, in the process of getting Old, while fully aware of Heisenberg's principle of indeterminacy.[2] (I didn't take Physics 101 twice for nothing.) He was correct, too. For instance, I've noticed that when I stop and remember, *My goodness, I'm OLD!* I tend to sit straighter and walk faster. That's because someone told me that when you walk faster you look younger.

2. The act of observation changes whatever is under observation.

Perhaps this is because when you're going fast, the pedal to the metal, not quite like a speeding bullet but as fast as you can — they don't have a chance to edit you line by line.

I've made some notes, too, of my own original reactions. Greatly to my surprise, I found they are not so original as I thought! Indeed, chatting with my peers, I've learned that we all say about the same things on getting off the trolley in Geriatricville and finding we missed the last car back. Accordingly, I thought I would list these remarks so no one will ever have to say them again.

1. **Can you believe it? How did we get to be this old?**
   But that's apt to happen, if you keep breathing in and out and showing up for meals.

2. **Oh well, you're as young as you feel.**
   Not so. Acting on that assumption can lead to elderly beach boys who need a B-cup bra, and mature ladies dancing the can-can. In truth, you're as young as your birth certificate indicates.

3. **But I feel like the same person!**
   Well, sure, doesn't everybody? Why would you suddenly start to feel like your next door neighbor?

4. You'll never catch me ending up in a nursing home!
   As if everyone else is clamoring to get into Eternal Vistas, where you can race around in your walker and fasten everything with Velcro and eat things you don't have to chew.

ॐ

By the way, you may have noticed how people tend to pussyfoot around the word "Old." They'd rather say Elderly. Or Older. But I want to know, Older than what? Sin? Mud? The hills? Or they will say Chronologically Challenged. I don't see anything the matter with Old.

It was at this point that the editor phoned me.

"Excuse me," he said, "but don't you think you should clarify this? That is, are you talking about Old? Or, well, *really* old?"

"I've thought about it a lot," I said finally, after a pause, "and I think people should decide for themselves which category they fit."

"But what are the categories?" he asked.

"So far as I know," I said, "there are only three. There's NSC — that stands for No Spring Chicken. And RWP — that's Really Well Preserved. And finally there's YLG — You're Looking *Great!*"

"Hmmmmm," the editor said.

~~

Whatever the category, it is an insidious process getting there. When you first come down with it, you hardly realize it's happening, because it is ever so gradual, rather like fudge in the process of becoming fudge. You beat it till it goes from thin-runny to thin-creamy to thick-creamy, and then comes the crisic moment when it is suddenly chocolate cement in the pan if you don't get it out of there fast. (This simile got away from me all of a sudden, and it didn't really work out. I'm going to come back and kick it around a little if I remember to.)

But time marches on, and presently we begin to have our suspicions. At least we've been acquiring more wrinkles[3] (known to Old Age apologists as Character Lines) till we seem to have more character than anybody needs. And once you start shedding your petals, you pick up speed and keep on shedding.

Speaking personally, I know I'm not young, because I don't have a Mohawk haircut, and I'm no good at computers, and I don't know the difference between a dork and a doofus and a dweeb. And I like you know, I mean, I talk like, you know, normal? And I never paid $75 for a bleacher seat to hear Si Kottik

---

3. There are three basic types: cockles, wrinkles, and furrows. "Cockles" is a word that got lost in the centuries, but I think it means those tiny, tiny lines the cosmetics ads are always talking about. "Wrinkles" are what don't look so bad by the light of a 10-watt bulb. The adds never mention "furrows," which are the kind you could plant corn in.

and his Running Sores. And I suspect I've departed the Middle Age Depot, because I am no longer peeved at those sentences in novels like, "*...and she knew her looks were going — after all, she was almost thirty....*" I only laugh hysterically. And I don't bother anymore to carve little butter balls when there are guests for dinner, and I don't wear my contacts half as much as my glasses. Oh, there are clues, all right, if you've been paying attention.

ॐ

Then when the Social Security checks start coming, you think, *How observant of the government!* Because even though you've noticed that some mornings you look like who-did-it-and-ran, you thought it was your own little secret. You're the same as you always were. As Garrison Keillor has pointed out, sometimes you just have to look reality in the eye and deny it. *Anyway, the light's bad in here. You didn't get much sleep last night. You never could wear yellow.* And so on.

But the evidence continues to pile up. Class reunions happen. Why did they let themselves get so old and funny-looking? Then you realize they don't recognize you either. Then you hear of some Old person living in an abandoned school bus with thirty-two mangy dogs and twenty-one scrawny cats, and you think, *Poor old thing,* and it turns out she's eight years younger than you are. This is not a warm fuzzy.

Neither are your birthdays, which seem to come along every few months, with thoughtful cards reminding you that the older you get, the better you were. And then some woman you'd swear could remember the Civil War gives you her seat on the bus. This is a real warning shot across the bow. You start conceding.

And then one day you have a clear-eyed moment of truth, a real slam-dunk epiphany, a defining moment, rather like the downy-cheeked soldier's on first hearing enemy gunfire,

Hey, they mean *me!*

This happened to me not long ago in a department store equipped with closed-circuit television. Glancing at it, I thought, *That's a pleasant-looking old couple over there,* and it turned out it was me and my husband I was admiring on the magic screen. And so I sidled up to the situation and really bit the bullet the next morning when the day's mail included a sale on cemetery lots.

I faced the mirror.

There it was, the personal knowledge of age and, like a backpack, I couldn't just shrug it off.

Breathes there a lass with soul so dead
She never to herself hath said,
  "That can't be me –
  It's Mother Machree!
I should have stood in bed."

Thus, eventually one settles in for the long, long trail a-winding, though one never knows just where or

Considering how fast they go, I'm not sure I want to know.

how far it's going to wind. The experts tell us that we are programmed, ideally, for 28,000 days. If you would divide that by 365, you would know how many years you have to live. This is assuming we start out with some good, sound genes and hardly ever get sick or run over or shot. But who can predict? And how much does one x-ray or case of sniffles subtract from the optimum number?

I've sometimes wondered if it wouldn't be better to be born with our individual expiration dates stamped on us somewhere, like cartons of milk at the supermarket. *Use before April 1, 1997.* You could live more sensibly. You wouldn't buy the jumbo box of cornflakes if you knew you had only five days to use it up. On the other hand, you might feel free to say Yes to whatever exciting adventure or project came along, if you knew there'd be ample time to enjoy it. But it wasn't planned that way.

However, not knowing is one of the interesting parts of getting Old. Whether that is a plus or a minus depends, I suppose, on your outlook. I tend to think there are more pluses than minuses in the whole picture, though I'm not entirely sure of that. Anyway, I will try to point them out as we go.

But this chapter is long enough now. I think I'll take a nap before going ahead, because I often find a nap helpful — a friendly green oasis in the middle of a day. Not that I'm sick or anything. I firmly believe it ain't over till it's over, and the Fat Lady hasn't sung yet, though recently I've heard her doing some warm-up warbling in the wings.

The classiest kind of an afternoon nap
Takes a comfortable couch and a cat on your lap.

Chapter Two

How You Look

They say, "Who cares?"
I disagree.
It matters quite
A bunch to me.

It goes without saying, as people say who are going to go ahead and say it anyway, we have hardly touched so far on the sensitive matter of falling apart. We have only discussed — for the benefit of others who may be getting old for the first time — how one eventually wakes to the sound of Time's winged chariot hurrying near, but not how or whether you can get out of the way.

This shouldn't be a long chapter, because there aren't too many options. If there were, the handsome young anchormen and weather girls on television wouldn't become ever so slightly saggy and shopworn with the passing years, nor would you have the chance to enjoy the nice warm feeling you get from the realization that the Beautiful People are mortal too. Therefore, we'll get it over now, so we can move on to jollier things.

Latest scientific finding: Older persons need reminding.

I'm mentioning what I plan to cover, because the Old

person often needs reminders of what's to be done. Otherwise the Old person is apt to take an off-ramp and never get back to the main highway. This is because of ADD, or Attention Deficit Disorder, which affects Old persons quite as often as the young. The young get Ritalin, and the Old get confused, as their attention keeps wandering from the subject at hand to matters more interesting. A brisk disconnect can happen without notice, and I think it's rather interesting that Henry VIII and Ann of Cleves apparently had the world's worst blind date. Some statesman had arranged the marriage before they even met, and when Henry saw how homely she was he had the statesman executed! Of course, you can't — wait a minute.

ॐ

"My memory and my brains have gone to wait for me somewhere else."
– Michelangelo

ॐ

Oh yes. As I was saying, it is essential to lay out a sort of map, in any sort of a guidebook, though this isn't really a guidebook. If you're on the way to somewhere for the first time yourself, how could you possibly guide someone else?

No, this book is simply a consideration of the situation from one woman's viewpoint, consisting of some good news, some useful rationalizations, and some comfortable old lies. Or, you might say, like a popcorn trail one might scatter through the forest in the hope that it might help someone in distress, if the squirrels don't get to it first.

TURN BACK THE ODOMETER
(OR, WHO SAID YOU CAN?)

It is natural for a woman to see her body and her face as her self, and when they become unfamiliar — the face in free fall, the earlobes longer, the hair scanty and blah-colored, she is in danger of disliking herself, which can lead to tantrums, too many highballs, and numerous sessions with the neighborhood shrink. She feels that this person looking back at her from the mirror is an interloper, and certainly no improvement on the original.

Disregard the way I look today –
You should have seen the girl that got away.

And the same with the body. When thin becomes thick, or slender becomes scrawny, and the skin changes from satin to seersucker, it is no wonder that she rises, as the trout to the fly, to bite on any new treatment that comes along.

I, myself, have a small jar of ivory-colored ointment that cost about the price of a small automobile. But so far I've had no feed-back, like, *What have you been doing; you look marvelous!* I think the small automobile might have been more fun. I also have a lipstick that contains optical diffusers, whatever they are, and free radicals protection. It still vanishes forty minutes after application and makes elegant stains on wine glasses and napkins. Mainly it proves that hope springs eternal.

My cells are trying valiantly,
They just forgot the recipe.

Incidentally, I learned the Facts of Lipstick only a few days ago. I had tried numerous brands, looking for one with staying power. Finally I found a guaranteed eight-hour lipstick and tried it. I learned that when they say "eight hours," they don't mean all at once. They just mean it will stay on for half an hour after you apply it, then another half-hour after you reapply it, and so on, until eventually it totals eight hours.

All this can be disconcerting, and probably more so for the woman who was a real beauty and has banked a good deal on her looks. The years inevitably nibble away at them, like mice at the cheese. Sometimes you can see where the cheese used to be, but this is small comfort, watching so much good cheddar go down the drain.

It isn't quite so painful when your looks are — so to speak — off the rack, but it is still dismaying. One must simply remember that sixty trillion body and face cells[4] have been loyally re-creating themselves for a good number of years, and that's enough to make anybody tired. So finally they give up and die, just as plants and fruitflies do, the difference being that plants and fruitflies don't write determinedly cheerful books about it, saying that beauty is in the character and so forth. But those sixty trillion body and face cells don't all quit together, but more or less one at a time. I often think it might be better if they'd all cooperate in one rollicking explosion, like the Fourth of July. But it wasn't planned that way.

☞

There are three main options for the Old or Older person who has finally knuckled under but is still concerned about it:

1   cover it up
2   change it
3   forget it

though the best approach is sometimes a shrewd mixture of them all, with the accent on Number 3.

☞

---

4. Who does all this counting?

In the interests of Keeping America Beautiful, Katharine Hepburn once said that the older you get, the more of yourself you should keep covered. (Living in sunny California, she must have seen enough uncovered people and body parts to last her for the foreseeable future.)

ↄ

Ordinarily you wouldn't expect to run into Katharine Hepburn and St. Francis of Assisi in the same chapter, but it's a small world. It was St. Francis who called his body Brother Ass, his body being that unruly part of himself that kept making unilateral decisions to do stupid things. Like falling down, or catching cold, or getting fat. I don't know whether or not St. Francis had a weight problem. But whatever his problems were, they were the fault of Brother Ass.

I think many of us feel that way. The body has a mind of its own. We all have a Brother Ass. Talk about three-day houseguests smelling like three-day-old fish! Brother Ass moves in with you the day you're conceived and stays for a lifetime. Moreover, the older we get, the more independent he gets, and the more stubborn. Which is why it becomes harder to shed pounds as the years go by.

ↄ

Much has been written about the Body Beautiful, but the 200-pounder in shorts just isn't. The big problem here with the Old person is that the birthday suit no longer fits well, and it can't be taken back for alterations. Our 200-pounder's is much too small, so it's filled to bursting. And if she gets a stern get-thee-to-a-diet-and-exercise-parlor directive from the doctor, perhaps she ought to. But it is to be hoped that she has the starch to stick with it for a matter of years. Which she probably doesn't because she loves to eat. A plump old friend told me candidly that she wasn't about to start dieting, because she didn't want her dying thought to be *"Dammit, why didn't I finish that peanut brittle?"*

Should anyone want to feel younger and thinner,
It's not a colossally difficult matter.
You needn't skip rope or your lunch or your dinner
Just hang with the crowd that is older and fatter.

Moreover, if she beats the odds and loses three dress sizes, she will undoubtedly acquire more wrinkles than ever. This is an excellent example of William Shapiro's Law of Unintended Consequences (like hitting a home run that wins the ball game but breaks a window).

As for Miss Anorexia of 1997, scrawny but smug in her teeny-weeny string bikini, and the aging 125-

pound lady in the playsuit, their aging skins nearly always become two sizes too big, so they look as though they'd been slept in. But gaining fifteen pounds will fill up the skin only in spots, precisely the wrong spots at that.

Upsizing isn't as easy as one would imagine, they tell me, but downsizing is even harder, when it comes to keeping the pounds off. My friend Sandy says she has lost and regained the same ten pounds so many times that she welcomes each one of them back by name. "Well, if it isn't Gertrude!" she'll say. "Hi there, Bonnie Sue, how ya doin'?"

But why should Sandy continue with such an unrewarding hobby? Unless she has reached critical mass — that is, when her family gets really critical and her friends keep telling her how well she looks, why can't she relax now? Because of the skinny twenty-year-olds in ads and on television, that's why. (Actually, though, people won't love Sandy any more or any less when she is ten pounds lighter, and it's good to remember the wise words of Nancy Reagan,

For this is the Law of the Mini,
As old and as true as the skies,
And valid from here to New Guinea:
They designed it for juvenile thighs.

who ought to know — "It is hard to like a woman who wears a size 6.")

And so these years might be called caftan time, muumuu-time, turtleneck time, midcalf skirt time, scarf time, long-sleeve time. But if you should, in spite of everything, go sleeveless, remember not to shake the salt.

Mainly, the SS&G look has to go. (Children, that's fifties talk for Sweet-Simple-and-Girlish.) The dirndl has to go, along with the Spandex tights and the huge sloppy top. The sorry fact is that young fashions do not make the Old person look like a young person, but only like an Old person who got into Teen Town by mistake.

ॐ

Back again for a moment to Hepburn. I've found that even, trying hard, I can't cover up everything. Florence Scott Maxwell noted when she was 84 that Old age is mainly a collection of infirmities you neglect to recover from — the blotch here, the ropy vein, the stiffened finger. Speaking of which, the hands: what do you do about them? You can't sit on them all the time, and it is hard to eat neatly with gloves on.

ॐ

I was given two tickets to an elegant fashion show, and I invited a friend to come with me. No, she said, she never went to fashion shows.

"Why not?" I asked.

"They make me feel old and ugly and fat and broke," she said. "Why do you go?"

"Well, it makes my feet feel good to watch the models teeter around in the high heels," I said. "I bet they can't wait to take them off."

Indeed, let's consider the feet. Many feet, especially older feet, aren't very pretty, because they were punished for too many years by four-inch heels on pointy-toed shoes.

Tell me, pray tell me,
If anyone knows
How did they make us pry these
Into those?

It was a trade-off. The calves of the legs are curvier and prettier in high heels, and so the models generally wear them on the runway. But when the show is over, they kick them off and put on Fashion's current idiotic fad, those clumsy clunky shoes that make Grandma's old Enna Jetticks look positively sexy. And so, as a comfortable compromise, the smart Old person wears flats or sports shoes like Reeboks or Nikes, which make feet look like horses'

hooves, but they are still not as ugly as Fashion's newest. Also, when she wears them, the Old person looks as though she might be heading for an aerobics workout, which is an in-thing to be doing, even though her only exercise may be rocking fast when she's mad.

ॐ

Hair, of course, poses its own problems and, again, the Hepburn dictum isn't too easily followed. You hear a great deal about the graying of America, but the graying isn't half so evident as the coloring. It used to be that only your hairdresser knew for sure. Now everyone probably does, and nobody cares. It is okay manners in most quarters to say, "I love your hair; who does your color?" And she probably won't mind if you switch to Strawberry Champagne yourself, though remember, on you it might look like Dr. Pepper.

And there are those who give their hair permission to go gray or white, whatever it wants to do. Often that's the best option, for the Old person who stays doggedly darkhaired or gold-blonde gets that Now-hair over a Then-face look. At a restaurant once, I overheard the headwaiter tell a busboy, "Take care of the dandelions in the corner, okay?" I looked over to the round table where six white-haired women were lunching, and they did look like off-season dandelions, a frothy white ring of them, and very pretty too.

Something else, hair-wise: it gets thinner. Why can't hair get thicker and waistlines thinner? But no, it's the other way around. The geriatric experts tell us we lose between 70 and 100 hairs a day after age thirty or thereabouts. No wonder Grandma saved it for pincushions and brooches. The way I've been shedding lately I'll shortly have enough for a mattress.

The question that's driving me bats,
Is "What ever happened to hats?"

Formerly you could hide all sorts of hair misery under a hat. But not anymore. Though there are thousands of hats around, they all seem to be in the shops, not on the heads.

⠀

Heavens to Betsy! and jeepers! and whee!
You'd never suspect that it's little old me!

Still, there are wigs! Indeed, there are wigs and wigs — good ones and bad ones, and when they are bad they are horrid. But wigs have improved vastly in the past few decades, and they needn't be the impossibly shiny curly bathing caps of yore that had you looking like Harpo Marx on a bad hair day.

I bought a wig a couple

of years ago, when I'd been sick and feeling those inti-
mations of mortality you feel when your temperature is
over 104. A big problem with being sick is that you
look as bad as you feel, but you can't get to the beauty
salon for the intensive care you need more than pills.
So you dislike yourself and — inevitably, therefore —
everyone else, and you're harder than ever to be
around. And so, when I was barely able to navigate, I
bought a wig from Brenda the Wig Lady, after which I
improved rapidly and so did my temper.

Remember, children, if Grandma gets totally
impossible, get her a wig.

A neighbor of mine has a wig she wears most of
the time, but she says she never feels quite at ease
wearing it until it starts looking like a roadkill, which is
how her own hair usually looks. So one wonders why
she bothers to put it on. But she feels better in it, she
says, and it keeps her head warm.

ᑐ

Which brings us finally
to the face, which is harder
than anything else to cover
unless you live in the
Middle East. (Here in
the Western world we
used to wear hats with
coquettish little veils, and
they were of considerable

Even a Syrian chador I think'll
Not cover completely a resolute wrinkle.

help. You'll find them mainly at theatrical costume places, if you like that just-stepped-out-of-the-forties look. Still, you'd have to have harlequin glasses and spanking-white gloves, and those glasses are hard to find.

Proper skin care seems to be the thing now and, by the way, it has certainly changed, as so many things have, since I was in the seventh grade. That was when all of us eleven-year-olds saved our allowances to buy — no, not tattoos — Tangee lipsticks. We sneaked some on, as soon as we left for school, worrying about our complexions and taking skin care very seriously.

A whole section in our hygiene book was devoted to it, but I remember mainly the part about The Pores. They keep opening and closing like tiny windows, we learned. Hot water opens them and cold water closes them. Therefore, at bedtime, one should wash the face with soap and hot water to get the little suckers clean, then rinse with cold water to shut them up. I never could understand how they could get full of dirt again, once you'd shut them up. But mine was not to reason why. Next, cold cream, and that was it.

No more, though. Now it takes four or five creams…I mean crèmes.[5] Periodically there is a great fanfare for something that obsoletes the rest — one totally perfect magical cream, the silver bullet, the Grail. This is it until next month's Grail. Still, they deserve an A for effort. As we all suspect, they are selling dreams and self-assurance, and most of us can

---

5. Advertising copy writers are heavily penalized if they don't spell cream crème.

I know that youth is fleeting   To find that I've been eating
But still it's rather trying   What I should have been applying.

use some more of each. Of course, you can buy it in other forms too, like booze, but cosmetics don't make you fat.

A good while ago when I was doing some TV commercials, I asked the makeup man for makeup advice. He had just finished doing makeup for *The Planet of the Apes,* so I thought he'd know what he was talking about.

He said that most women make the mistake of trying to look younger (this was news?), when they should be aiming for simply better. "Throw out your purple lipsticks. Old," he said. "You want bright scarlets." (I though of my friend Mary and me, some years ago, ruefully agreeing that we hadn't been transformed, even though our new lipsticks were named Cute Tomato.)

"But what if you're wearing something sort of purple?" I asked.

"Don't," he said. These fellows are all opinionated. He'd also told me that the Eleventh Commandment was: Never wear blue eye shadow. Ridiculous! Moses couldn't have known a thing about eye shadow.

And then he went on to say that we tend to continue using the makeup we used when we were — so to speak — at peak performance. For instance, anyone left over from the Clara Bow[6] era favors the Cupid's bow mouth. This rang a bell with me. I remembered sporting a Joan Crawford mouth for a number of years till eyes came back, with Elizabeth Taylor, I think. (Ankles to elbows to earlobes, you never know which body or face part is going to be featured next.) However, the Crawford mouth was a big rectangular one, wine-dark in a chalk-white face. I always thought my face tended to vanish without that mouth as a focal point, and half the time I wished it would anyway.

ॐ

My daughter, growing up in the Joan Baez years, wore no makeup at all, as did most of her contemporaries. I mentioned this to Steve-the-makeup-man, and he said he was in favor of that for the under-twenties with good skin color or the tanned outdoor look.

---

6. She was known as The IT Girl, children, a long time ago.

"It's the honest WYSIWYG approach," he said, and I said, "What's that?" because I didn't have a computer then.

"What You See Is What You Get," he said, putting a dab of something on my nose to make it look shorter. "You see it a lot on the old flower children from the sixties. They've probably thrown away their love beads, but they really hang onto the Nature Girl look. Only they're older now, and they've more or less lost the good skin color or the tan, so it's more the half-dead look. They ought to do something."

"Like what?" I asked.

"Like cover it up." (Here we are again, I thought.) "With a good foundation, but not too coppery or you get that Pocahontas effect. And listen," he continued, "if you ever write about any of this, for Pete's sake, tell 'em not to stop with the face; go under the chin with it and up to the ears." So I promised, and there it is. Under the chin it goes, and the shirt collar be damned.

꒛

The second option is plastic surgery (or what you might call the cutting edge of facial rejuvenation). Often it rejuvenates to a quite satisfactory degree, if you have the right kind of skin and a truly expert surgeon.[7] The basic eye and face job will buy you half

---

7. Check his credentials. Ask to talk to a few clients and see their before-and-afters.

a dozen years of looking better than you do right now. But you can't do it too often. When Mae West said too much of a good thing was wonderful, she wasn't talking about face-lifts.[8]

From what I have observed, structural remodeling is nearly always a happy improvement — adding on to the under-chinned person or subtracting from the overly nosed. These additions (or subtractions) are a more lasting investment than the all-over tightening up — have a longer self life, you might say, though you probably shouldn't.

It is true that some people are philosophically against these surgical assists, or perhaps they can't afford to have it done themselves.

"Go with what you've got," they say. "Age gracefully. Be natural!"

What's so great about Natural? you might think. Warts are natural too, but who wants any?

An 82-year-old friend of mine decided to buy herself some nips and tucks. Her daughter said that at her age it would just be rearranging the deck chairs on the *Titanic*. My friend told her daughter to pipe down, and did it anyway. She was quite happy with the results.

And so you might add together the prices of the palliatives we've mentioned...

---

8. "I saw Sophia Loren — the Italian woman with those wonderful cheekbones — in a movie the other day. She must have had 24 face-lifts, and she looked like an alien, as if she weren't from this world at all. Her Italian wrinkles would have been a thousand times more beautiful."
– Robert Bly.

- a good expensive surgical job
- some good-looking cover-up clothes
- a good wig
- an industrial-strength diet-and-exercise program

...and while you're at it, get the figures on a First Cabin Total Luxury Cruise to anywhere in the world you want to go. Add up the numbers. Then check the credit limits on your credit cards, get some more credit cards, and go for the works. I know a woman who did just that, because she wanted to have something not to tell her grandchildren. I believe she omitted the diet-and-exercise part, though, because it didn't sound like fun.

So do it now — no point hanging around debating. Do it now, that is, unless you decide to go for the third choice:

Forget it.

You can lean back and settle comfortably into who you are, once you get that figured out. Which is an appealing prospect too.

Chapter Three

The Comfort Zone

Few joys are joys at every age;
I know one only, which is
Of equal joy to tot or sage –
Scratching where it itches.

"I *have been thinking about old age and how much I enjoy the freedom of it. By that I mean the freedom to be absurd, the freedom to forget things because everyone expects you to forget, the freedom to be eccentric, if that is what you feel like, or, on the other hand, the freedom to be quite rigid and say, 'But this is the way I do things.'"*
                                        – May Sarton

ॐ

It is always a pleasure to find that someone else already said what you intended to say, but said it better, so you don't have to. I ran across these words quite recently, and I agree with every one of them.

After lunch the other day at The Petrified Pony[9], my friend said, "Let's have another cup of coffee," and I said, "Why not?" So we did. And I thought, because this book was on my mind, what a change from the

---

9. The week before, we'd tried The Quilted Giraffe. All the In restaurants have that sort of name now, and I think the SPCA should be told about it.

(want to get there before the kids do) or back to the office (Old Wotzisname hates long lunch hours) or back into the car (have to pick up somebody and deposit him somewhere for something — basketball practice, tennis, swimming, dancing...).

My friend was apparently thinking along the same lines.

"It's the world's best-kept secret, isn't it?" she said thoughtfully. "How nice it is."

"How nice what is?" I said.

"Just being the age we are," she said.

Her words stuck in my mind. I knew what she meant, and I also wanted to say, Yes, because I remembered how I felt as a teenager about Old persons, if indeed I thought about them at all. Poor old things about says it. We had no idea that they had — well, real lives. It was certainly a secret well kept from the teens, all right.

Then, as I was stirring my coffee and thinking maybe I'd order one of their good fudge-frosted brownies to go with it, my inner screen flashed back to a wind-whipped school hockey field and my fifteen-year-old self standing on it, hating the gummy feel of the taped hockey stick handle and praying the ball[10] wouldn't come my way. I'm sure the rest of the team was praying the same thing. They knew I wouldn't know what to do with it, and they were right; I never did.

---

10. It was a ball, not a puck, in field hockey, though it sounds funny in these days of ice hockey. It was a very hard ball and hurt like the devil when it banged into your shins.

And I remember how the other part of my mind was miserably worrying about the pink bump on my chin. It was on its way to becoming a world-class pimple, just in time for Saturday night's school hop. But who cared, I thought grimly. I was only going with Shorty Dekins, a fat-faced kid who undoubtedly hated the prospect as much as I did.... Oh, those joyous fun-filled days of youth!

I called the waitress over. "I'll have one of those good brownies," I told her. You don't get pimples when you're an Old person.

"Me too," said my friend.

We agreed that we wouldn't trade our age for my granddaughter's — she will be fifteen next week. We also agreed that my granddaughter and her peers would undoubtedly be surprised to hear it.

ॐ

Yes indeed. It's a good age to be, in spite of some drawbacks. But on the other hand — and there's always an other hand — how one feels about it depends to a considerable extent on fortune. Outrageous fortune, perhaps, and what particular slings and arrows she may have saved up just for you. It depends so much on health and finances and the people you love and what happens to them.

We all know people who have been practically leveled by some of the landmines of the later years. They are living, if you can call it that, with more pain and distress than anyone should be asked to live with. Living with loneliness can be heartbreaking, as is the searing grief of outliving your true love or your children, which should never happen in a just world (but whoever said it was?).

How you feel about aging depends heavily on something else, too, I thought: on how you feel about your own Self and whether you've found it yet, to exhume a good old psychological cliché.

I can remember back, some decades ago, when "Go chase yourself" was a genial and popular putdown. But it is phrased more politely these days. "Decode yourself!" "Solve your identity crisis!" "Make friends with your inner child!" "Find the real You!" Or, back to Square One, "Go chase yourself."

At any rate, talking about it was a popular pastime even when I was in college, back before the flood of self-help books that spilled over the country in the late sixties and kept on spilling. Much amateur soul-searching was going on. We didn't know then how long it would take a lot of us to figure out who we were — after all, so little trustworthy evidence was in — or what to do about it when we did.

~

I caught a bad case of Who-Am-I in my junior year. One fresh April morning I started hitchhiking, with nothing but a ten-dollar bill, a toothbrush, and a book of Browning's poems for a roadmap. Classes and campus could go hang, I didn't care. I didn't care where I was going, either. I was going to find myself.

A chicken farmer driving a rusty old pickup truck gave me a lift. People weren't so suspicious then. Luckily he was a nice fatherly type who must have had a nineteen-year-old daughter himself, he was that concerned. "Go back to school," he told me firmly when he let me out, some forty miles down the road. I nodded and thanked him but kept on going, another hundred miles or so. Catching rides was easy.

Nothing bad happened to me, which goes to prove that His eye is on the sparrow, or at least on the bird-brain. But somewhere along Route 66 — that's when there was a Route 66 — I had some second thoughts. How long would ten dollars last me? (Longer than it would today, I can tell you, but still, not forever.) More important, what if I found myself and also found I wasn't worth looking for? Maybe ignorance was bliss. Better be safe than sorry.

A few hours later it was good to be back in the dorm.

～

I didn't learn for years that you generally find your Self after you quit looking for it. And that your Self gets put together in spite of you, after you've lived awhile. Or, you might say, after the various selves you've lived through get stacked up, then firmly pressed together.

This is known to psychologists as the Club Sandwich Postulate. More accurately, it isn't known to psychologists yet, but it will be as soon as I explain it to them.

Everyone, you see, consists of eight layers — often even more, in the case of the Old person. You have your

> bread[11]
> bacon
> tomato
> turkey
> lettuce
> mayonnaise
> butter
> bread[12]

in a neat stack. This is then put into a compactor. You remember the kitchen compactors that virtually obsoleted themselves by being too good at what they did? They compressed enormous heaps of stuff into a smallish superheavy and unbiodegradable brick. (I don't know if any compactors are still around, and I'd be amazed if the trash-collectors are, after the hernias and heart attacks they were getting from picking up those heavy bricks.)

And that is what the years do — add layers and compress them all together, each one present and part of the whole, adding its own particular flavor or texture. Talk about the Child Within! There's the Teen

---

11. Toasted or not, whichever. I prefer toasted.
12. Ditto.

Within, the student, the prude, the hell-raiser, the father or mother, the CEO.... Every sandwich differs, of course, because we've all led different lives. And with all these inputs from all these little selves, it's no wonder you sometimes surprise yourself by the way you act or react. And no wonder it can take a good while to get a realistic picture of who it is you've been going steady with for so long.

I've noticed, myself, that each of my selves usually regarded the self it just passed with — at best — amused condescension. (Then? I was just a dumb bunny. But now I'm in the fifth grade!) Or later, perhaps between jobs, floundering around like a boneless chicken, (Why didn't I have enough brains to stick with it?) (Why didn't I shoot the guy?) (Why didn't I get a degree?) (Why didn't I run away and join the circus?) (Why didn't I... whatever!!)

But it's wrong to be too harsh with any of those Selves. You still have them with you, and they deserve the benefit of the doubt. They were probably doing the best they could at the time, considering what they had to work with. And in giving herself a report card, which the Old person is entitled to do at this stage of the game,

Don't be mean to the child you were You can't get rid of him (or her).

Keeping them all is a cinch, my dears,
Locked in a trunk, they'll keep for years.

she'd better grade kindly. Too, she'd better let go of most of the garbage she's been carrying around,[13] if any, so she can think about more interesting things.

I'm all right now. And looking back, if you find as I did that you hitched your wagon to a star that never stopped receding, welcome to the Club. We're mostly friendly people, we Old persons who winged it through most of a lifetime — is there any other way to do it? — and find it was a pretty good trip. We worked some and played some, helped some Boy Scouts across the street, fastened our seatbelts, took our vitamins, paid our way, voted, stayed out of jail, and hope we did more good than harm.

So here we are in the Comfort Zone — the more comfortable because we know ourselves a bit and know what to expect of ourselves. Remember when you thought you'd really follow through with the New

---

13. I'm aware that some people can't. I know a man who is stuck with an enormous bundle of hate for his father for no discernible reason. Poor Walt trudges endlessly through the somber forests of his childhood, going over and over the same sorry trails that lead nowhere, but he can't put that bundle down. His father. His father. It would take a team of psychiatrists working night and day to get him away from it, and he'd fall down if they did, it's been a prop for so long. For then he'd have to blame himself.

Year's resolves? And, by extension, we know better
what to expect of other people. In fact, most of us Old
persons have learned that a cheerful healthy skepticism
in many areas makes life more comfortable all around,
because there are fewer disappointments. We don't
believe much anymore in seed catalogs, dress sizes,
moisturizers, fast recipes, political candidates, book
jacket blurbs, and quite a few other things.

꒰꒱

Adele Starbird[14] recalls with what pleasant antici-
pation she had looked forward to old age. "I shall relin-
quish my lifelong struggle to remember names. I shall
say frankly, 'My dear, I haven't the faintest idea who
you are. But you are very pretty. Do sit down and talk
to me if you can stand it.'" And then, when she finally
got there, she wrote, "I find old age even more
delightful than I dreamed it could be. The absence of
pressure and competition, the independence, the
spacious feeling of leisure...."

꒰꒱

Spacious. That's the word I've been looking for.
Looking back over the young years, the middle
and later years, I seem to be looking at a patchwork
quilt — bright patches and gray, rotten ones and

---

14. Columnist and onetime Dean of Women at Washington University
in St. Louis, Missouri.

wonderful ones, but all of those years constricted by deadlines and duties and dates and schedules, everything timed by the clock or the calendar.

And now it isn't. It seems odd that life should seem spacious to me now, when there can't be a great deal of it left. Yet it does. Perhaps it is what William Styron calls somewhere, "the pooping out of ego and ambition." Perhaps they occupied more space in my psyche than ever I realized, and made those rigid boundaries necessary, as well as those micro-managed minutes.

But not now. Now I've been served this lavish dollop of Discretionary Time — leisure time I thought I'd never see, back in the more harried days. The danger is that when you have those lovely unoccupied leisure hours at your disposal, dark forces are waiting to fill them up with Worthwhile Leisure Activities. (Don't I ever get time to stand and stare?)

Spacious. That's the feeling. A time to pause, regroup, breathe easy, and look around. That's the feeling. Been there, done that, don't have to do it again. So many things you do in a lifetime are Exhilarating or Fun or Worthwhile or Gratifying, or any of a dozen other good adjectives, but not Habit-forming. When I see a gaggle of teenagers, I find it blissful to realize I'm not raising one. When I see a family set out for the Fourth of July beach picnic, I happily wave to them. May their beer remain cold and their hot dogs sand-free and the kids sweet-tempered, and may their potato salad be better than the kind Aunt Carrie used to bring to ours.

Sometimes it seems to me that there is a conspiracy afoot — a Commie plot? — to make us Old persons stop doing things we enjoy and start doing things we don't. No law says you have to enjoy weaving potholders or building birdhouses down at the Senior Center. No law says you have to join every group in sight, or Get Involved

Under the broad and starry sky,
Pitch me a tent and let me lie
Here in my own backyard, alone —
Me and my cellular telephone.
No fear of curious strangers coming,
And happily close to some indoor plumbing.

(this is always pronounced with Capital Letters) if Getting Involved isn't your cup of tea. No law says you have to love camping in the great outdoors next to the Porta-Potty.

Buckminster Fuller, the famous builder and designer, creator of the geodesic dome, once said that the main thing, in the latter years, is to do what you most loved to do before the world said you had to get out there and make a living. What he meant, I am sure, is to pick up and continue your major childhood interest, on a more sophisticated level. I'll bet when he was a little boy he made superb paper airplanes.

It is important to remember that these are your Declining Years, in which you can jolly well decline to do what you don't feel like doing, unless not doing it would make you feel worse than doing it.

You can decline to finish the book that bored you witless by the end of the second chapter, even though

the friend who loaned it to you said it was the best thing
since Shakespeare. When did it start, this nonsense
about finishing things? Some things should never have
been started, let alone finished.

You can decline to look for items you misplace.
Let them find you. It simplifies life enormously to have
three of everything that's important to the daily round,
like eyeglasses or car keys or canes or umbrellas.

You can decline to go to huge cocktail parties full
of people you don't know or particularly care to.

You can decline to sign up for sweaty workouts
somewhere. You can decline to buy a rowing machine.
I find I get enough exercise hustling to the other end of
the house to retrieve something or do something, then
skidding to a halt as I realize I haven't the faintest
notion what I was going to retrieve or do, then
chugging back to where I started from — that's
what I have to do to remember it again — and doing
a fast repeat.

It's good to remember, as well, that these are also
the Permissive Years. Of course, they're permissive for
everybody else, witness the fat slob in dirty jeans and
baseball cap at Pierre's last night, where you went for
your hundred-dollar Anniversary Dinner. Or the toddler
with the indelible crayons drawing choo-choo trains on
the tablecloth, to the accompaniment of his mother's
helpless, "Oh, Dougie, that was naughty!" And they are
permissive years for Old persons too.

Indeed, this particular decade of this particular
century is certainly the most comfortable time in
history to be Old, whether we're talking sports activities,

social graces, or science. You can bungee-jump or scuba-dive, if you'll sign a no-fault insurance form first. Or go for the Senior Olympics, or get a mudbike and head cross-country, and no one will call you crazy; they'll say you're wonderful.

Social-wise, you can go ethnic anywhere, in a sari or a muumuu or a caftan, if it is more comfortable, and who cares if you look like a refugee from the sixties. People will only assume you're hiding a truss or a brace, and they'll hope you're comfortable.

Also, being an Old person, you can dine at a friend's house and leave immediately after dinner, claiming charter membership in the International Eat-and-Run Society. (This will probably start a general exodus, and the hostess will be grateful.) And if you never wanted to go to the dinner anyway, you can simply not show up, then do an "Oh, was it this Thursday? I'm so embarrassed!" when the hostess telephones. This happens often enough anyway, and she'll probably not suspect a thing, inasmuch as we Old persons are notoriously dimwitted.

And speaking of foods you're not familiar with — I mean the weird things you can encounter anywhere, like ostrich steaks and baby kangaroo (they seem to be aborting everything these days), the Old

In chic cafes they overdo the fancy food and liquors.
"Pardonnez-moi, mais avez vous des Twinkies ou des Snickers?"

person can leave them alone and it will surprise no one. Even if you can digest nails, you're expected to have rather a frail and unadventurous stomach.

And, of course, you can live with a man or woman you aren't married to, known to the IRS as your POSSLQ (Person of Opposite Sex Sharing Living Quarters, and pronounced Posselcue). And you may, of course, without producing a marriage license, travel with your POSSLQ, in which case it becomes your POOSSCC (Person of Opposite Sex Sharing Cruise Cabin, pronounced Poosk).

It would seem to be Science that has contributed the largest measure of comfort to the Old person, in purely practical ways. I love their recent discoveries about our built-in Happiness Meter — that we are born with a happiness or misery level in place, and whether we win the Sweep-stakes or lose the farm makes little difference to our lasting overall set of mind and mood. If you were born three drinks behind (to borrow a good phrase of John Medina's), you'll stay that

ME AND MY BLUE GENES

Hooray for the wonders of Science!
From guilt we are suddenly free!
If I'm moody and mean
It's the fault of a gene,
And you'd better not blame it on me.

way, regardless. I can't quite believe it, myself. But what a good excuse for frequent tantrums when you're too old for PMS.

And, true, many of our aches, pains, and general miseries, including the mental variety, have been ameliorated if not obliterated by science, with its fantastic research facilities and new surgical techniques. If you truly can't stand yourself, or if other people can't, Prozac may give you a new personality, just as surgery can give you a new nose.

But I do wish they would stay out of the kitchen for awhile. Doesn't Science ever sleep? Now they've taken the fun out of food by declaring everything that tastes good off limits. Chicken? SALMONELLA! Bacon? NITRATES! Fish? MERCURY! Eggs? CHOLESTEROL! Cake? CALORIES! Drinking water? LIFE-THREATENING MINERALS! And how do you know your broccoli isn't full of PESTICIDES?

Sex Increases Body's Output of "Happy Making" Endorphins, Says Scientist

Surely here's the sharpest mind that Science yet has seen!
Any day I believe he'll find that grass is often green.

What they do — those scientists, I mean — is give a rat a chunk of cornbread, and if he has a headache that week, they tell us to stop eating cornbread. But we are fatalists, a lot of us Old persons. We tend to think we've made it to this age anyway, eating all those terrible things. Please pass the butter.

It is my candid opinion that Science spends most of its time working on the wrong things. They are either telling us something we already know, or something we don't want to know, or something they'll change their minds about tomorrow. I know Science will be devastated to hear that I feel like this, but that's the way it is, as we plunge bravely forward to the next chapter.

Chapter Four

Looking Back A Little

Twinkle, twinkle, little light
Blinking on and off all night.
Twinkle, twinkle, little star
Can someone fix my VCR?

August Andante

Regretfully the sun leaves, and dark comes late.
The soft shadows deepen now, along about eight,
And through the open window with the scent of warm
     clover
Comes the sound of Jane's piano just a green yard over.

Listen — that's a scale now; she crosses hands here,
And now a little tune starts, halting, shy, clear...
Rondo? Memories of Love? Elegy? Romance?
Or possibly a chorus of *The Primrose Dance?*

Summer isn't locusts, and shrill bright heat,
And the hot sun strumming with a harsh gold beat.
It's little cool piano notes, falteringly sweet
As gentle petals falling
       through a dusky summer twilight
           down a quiet summer street.

ॐ

Keep listening. Or, as we say now, stay tuned. But

I'm afraid you won't hear Jane's piano. The neighbor on the left is running his power mower (you won't hear the summery whirrr of the old-fashioned lawnmower either). And that spine-curdling earsplitting shriek is the neighbor on the right, using his leaf-blower from hell. And the boy across the street found an old *NYPD* rerun on the tube — BANG! BANG! — lots of bloody bodies in this one. Those little cool piano notes wouldn't have a chance, if there were any, but Jane isn't taking piano now. She traded her Barbie collection for a set of drums.

Yes, but on the other hand, I reminded myself, the neighbor on the left is getting his grass cut in a jiffy so he won't have to miss the school board meeting, as my daughter pointed out, when I was muttering about the noise. And tomorrow the right-hand neighbor's back won't be aching from raking, thanks to that devilishly efficient state-of-the-art leaf blower. And the boy across the street is at least home this evening, said my grand-daughter, who knows him —

I can no longer
  Tell time at a glance.
Is it twenty till June?
  Or a quarter to France?

not cruisin' for a bruisin' in the shady end of town. So I quit muttering, at least out loud.

ॐ

I've decided that one of the very good things about being an Old person is that you can enjoy most of the modern conveniences of our affluent Western society (even if you're not especially affluent) and at the same time wallow in warm memories of how nice it was before you had the modern conveniences, known in real estate parlance as the Mod Cons. (These days we have to shorten everything. Speed it up!)

Take, for example, air conditioning. Time was, hot summer nights, you sat on the front porch with a fan — not electric, probably — no outlets on front porches. And you'd talk, and count the cars going by, or count how many Fords. Or Chevys. (Now I can't tell one from another.) And maybe a neighbor would stop by and visit. And maybe somebody mentioned ice cream, and a kid would be dispatched to the drugstore (no freezer in the kitchen, of course; hardly a Mod Con in the place). And so the evening would turn into a real swinger, and then you'd go upstairs to bed and wish you were dead as you simmered and broiled and steamed and prayed for a breeze and roamed around till dawn trying to find one.

These days I don't know the names of the neighbors[15]. And we don't have a front porch, though

---

15. Today the neighbors live mostly on the gently curving screen of the TV set, and they are the news anchors or weather or talk-show or sitcom people. We'd recognize them in a minute, but probably not the people down the block, or in the neighboring condo.

there's plenty of Pecan Ripple in the freezer. And if you take away our air-conditioning, it will be over my lifeless form.

And still I look fondly back to that livable-in-spite-of-everything era, which is something the young person cannot do. He is royally stuck in the here and now, with no other time frame to roam around in.

The other day I was giving some bulb-planting instructions to Howie, the fifteen-year-old who does odd jobs around the yard. He nodded wisely. "I know where you're coming from," he shouted over his blasstissimo boombox that seems to be umbilically attached. (If only it would play a recognizable tune once in awhile, something you could hum! I know Lawrence Welk would agree with me, too.)

Well, I looked at Howie, in grungy acid-washed jeans my generation wouldn't have worn to a mudfight, and the baseball cap on backwards, and the T-shirt that said MAKE LOVE, NOT BABIES, and I thought, No, you don't, Howie. You don't know where I'm coming from, any more than I know where you're coming from.

Sometimes I think it isn't a generation gap; it's a chasm.

I grew up in a safe and likable and fairly innocent kind of a world, or anyway, most of us thought so at the time. It was a Norman Rockwell kind of a world,[16] as it looked on the covers of *The Saturday Evening Post* (with — somehow — echoes of *Seventy-six Trombones* somewhere in the picture). And we had national heroes and national villains, and it was easy to tell them apart, and all this was reflected in our wholesome juvenile literature too.

As I remember, policemen were gruff-but-kindly twinkly types, and schoolteachers were maiden ladies you wouldn't dare talk back to, and the school principal — Wow! Stay out of *his* way. And Holland was populated by plump, rosy people all wearing wooden shoes, and Mexicans wore huge sombreros and slumped against adobe walls in the hot sunshine. And all families ate dinner together at home every night, and nice girls DIDN'T and bad girls DID. And $10,000 a year was a lot of salary, and a good-sized candy bar cost a nickel.

Yes, and blusher was rouge, and moisturizer was cold cream, and pasta was spaghetti in tomato sauce, and women still darned the family socks, and remote was an adjective, not a noun, and it was Add-a-Pearl for little girls, not Add-a-Barbie. And strawberries in January were a treat instead of a yawn, and a corset was a corset, not a tummy-tamer, and it was slums, not Inner City. And they had not yet invented the infomer-

---

16. I didn't tell Howie that. He wouldn't know Norman Rockwell from Knute Rockne, but he wouldn't know Knute Rockne either.

cial, and nobody ever said veggies. And people fell in love, not into relationships, and you didn't say wellness, you said Good Health, and if you happened to lose it, you called the family doctor, who came trudging up the walk, sturdy black bag swinging, and you felt better fast.[17]

སྱ

But back to Howie, who probably has the bulbs in by this time.

Hi-Tech Toys Outsell Stuffed Goods, 2 to 1

I can't deny the merits of
High-tech – it's great, it's new –
But what's to take to bed and
love?
O Raggedy Ann! O Pooh!

Indeed, there is a distance between his world and mine. And it isn't that I haven't been paying attention. It's just that I've been busy doing the things you do — family, jobs, kids, watering the aspidistra, all that — till suddenly one fine morning there comes the overdue revelation. *Toto, I've a feeling we're not in Kansas anymore.* Yet a part of me still is. In some foggy impressionistic sort of way, it continues to believe all those

17. The other day I didn't feel so great, and I telephoned my HMO. It said, "Your call will be answered as soon as the Advice Nurse for your Health Care Provider's module is available. Please stay on the line." I listened to the standby music awhile and then took two aspirin.

things I just mentioned. All that and a whole lot more is the residual baggage I carry around with me in spite of myself, because it is what I was imprinted with at a very impressionable age.

Howie, on the other hand, is a space-age-TV-high-tech product, and I can't visualize his interior landscape. What sort is it? What kind of imprints? Different from mine, certainly. We could hail from different countries. In the third grade I was mired in the Gazintas, like 3 gazinta 12 four times. Howie probably never saw a Gazinta; he had a calculator, and he was talking RAMs, ROMs and space flights, as well as taking a Computer Studies Enrichment course at summer camp.

And, of course, his points of reference are different. Back when the generations teethed on more or less the same culture, there was a handy conversational shorthand. Mention Tom Mix, Mayor LaTrivia, Ferdinand smelling the flowers, or Camille in the third act, and he would probably say, "Huh?" As I would if he mentioned (I asked my granddaughter what to put in here) Marky Mark.

In a word, he feels easy with the past decade and a half, having grown up in it, while I (as we'd have put it in the forties) am a little nervous in the service.

He is probably unshockable, too, by all the naughty words sprinkled like poppyseeds in a poundcake through magazines we've always kept in plain sight, but now we're not sure we should. Because of my cultural residue, I find that I'm always a bit jolted, not by the words themselves, but by where you find them: in the mouths of freewheeling toddlers. Or when I see magazines once devoted to molded salads and needlework things now featuring articles like *25 New Ways to Please Your Sex Partner.*[18]

And while we're in this steamy part of the greenhouse, how about the way they kiss in the movies? Just open their mouths and start chewing each other up. Claudette Colbert never kissed that way, nor Bogart and Bacall. And when they coupled, it was behind closed doors, and for all we knew, they were just necking (I guess no one necks anymore) and planning the wedding.

But it is probably the high-tech and/or cybernetic aspects of the worlds we carry in our heads that mainly differentiate Howie and me. He is a native-born citizen of the cybernetic world, while I am still waiting for my naturalization papers, as are a good many of my peers.

I know as much about the cyber-world as the next person, if the next person happens to be a total chump. I am keyboarding this now, and you will never know at what cost to my self-esteem and temper, learning even this much. I found that you have to know something about it before you can learn anything about it, if you follow me — same principle that applies to cleaning the house at least a little before the housecleaner comes. But being a writer, I've had to learn the minimum, because you don't mail a hefty typewritten manuscript in a box these days, when you've written a book. Editors want your words on a disk, and they take

18. Not husband, mind you, or wife. Boss? Mailman? St. Bernard?

it from there. (It isn't as though this is the first computer-word-processor I ever had. I bought one in 1982, and it is, to this one, as the tricycle is to the Concorde.)

ॐ

    But let me go back a bit. Office equipment wasn't always so hard to master. For instance, the paper clip. It didn't take me long to get the idea there, and I caught onto the pencil sharpener real fast too. Then came my first manual typewriter, and I still didn't panic — even learned eventually how to change the ribbon and keep the striker keys clean. (Whatever happened to bobby pins?)

Back in a simpler,
More leisurely day,
How happy I was,
Just typing away!

    Now, right here is where we see the future shining a great white spotlight on an important scientific principle:

**The older you get, the more complicated
the things you have to work with.**

Comes now the electric typewriter!

At first, I missed the busy, authoritative sound of keys being solidly struck. And my touch was too heavy, a lead foot on the gas pedal. A heavy touch on the electricccccccccccc made it go like that. But I eventually lightened up, so it was okay except when it went ballistic and started typing garbage I hadn't even written, I mean the %##**&+@*$% kind of garbageeeeeeeeee. Of course, I couldn't repair it myself — all those little tiny parts? — and I'd have to schlepp it over to the electrical genius across the river and down the pike. Seven days and a hundred bucks later I would retrieve it.

And then came the computer, or word processor. (Every WP is a computer, they tell me, though every computer isn't a WP, unless I have it backwards. Ask somebody who knows.) Because right now, the world is divided into two kinds of people: knowledgeable, enthusiastic computer nerds, and people who'd rather pretend it never happened. (No, three kinds, if you count people like me, with one toe in the water, wondering what to do next.)

ॐ

The editor happened to look over my shoulder at this point, and he said, "Don't you think you might as well leave the whole subject alone, if you're going to brush it off like that? At least till you finish this book?"

And I said, "I don't see how I can. It's on my mind so much of the time, like whether I'll ever be able to find Chapter Two again. That's the one I wanted to add to, but I don't know where my word processor put it."

"That's okay, you can always rewrite it, no problem," the editor said.

Yeah, right, I thought. Editors are like that.

"Isn't there anything you like about computers?" he asked.

I considered. "Well, I like some of the computer-talk abbreviations. I mean acronyms, or whatever they are," I conceded. "Like HHOK. There's a list of them in the back of my computer book."

"What's that stand for?" he asked.

"Ha Ha Only Kidding," I said.

"Hmmmmm," the editor said.

A neighbor who recently bought a computer telephoned the other day, asking where my computer's parallel port is. I don't know whether this fellow is walking the walk or just talking the talk, though I suspect he doesn't know much more about it than I do. I wasn't about to

It's abundantly clear
That I don't belong here.

admit that I didn't know I had a parallel port, so I said, "Come on over and see for yourself."

"Be there in a mouse-click," he said cheerily, and showed up half a minute later.

Just to get even, I asked him how many applications he had in his CD ROM — I'd picked that up from an ad and thought it sounded good. He didn't know, so I felt better. He still knows more than I do, I'm sure, but I didn't want to start any conversations.

My friend Eloise, looking at this chapter, said, "You didn't mention the time you panicked and the repairman found you hadn't turned the thing on."

"I'm not about to mention it, either," I said.

Another point: has the computer really improved communications? Computer Boobs and Computer Nerds don't mingle much, because they tend to bore each other spitless. There are more computer-widows and widowers now than golf ditto, one person out buying new programs, the other taking endless, expensive computer courses so he/she won't feel like an alien in an incomprehensible land.

∽

There was another page to this chapter, about computer classes. It was to go right here, but it went somewhere else. Or, rather, the computer put it somewhere else. When I hit the FINDER and SEARCH keys and all that, two cute frolicking dachshunds appeared on the magic screen, singing,

We're happy little puppy dogs,
We love to run and play...

It turned out it was the start of the little neighbor girl's third-grade exhibit project. She was playing in my office while her mother and I chatted in the other room.

Your typewriter would never do that to you.

చ౿

At any rate, I've wondered, as well, whether or not the WP has improved the quality of the writing that's being communicated. Computer nerds will say, "Oh, certainly! It's so easy to shift and delete and revise." And I say, "Yes, but how much revising is really done in your basic dumb business letter — 'Yrs of the 17th inst. rec'd and in reply would say...'"

As for writers, does their output improve, literarily speaking? Does their language have enough marination in the mind beforehand, when it flows so easily onto the screen, through the printer and onto the disk or paper? The process is so fluid (they tell me) that it is tempting to run on and on.[19]

I wonder how some of the sturdy old classics would read today. If Herman Melville had used a WP, would *Moby Dick* be a better book? Or just longer? As a card-carrying English major, I always felt that *Moby Dick* was quite long enough. But with a WP, would

---

19. "I have noticed, by the way, a tendency to ramble on this thing. Blah blah blah blah blah." – Betty Rollin, author.

Melville have been tempted to lengthen that splendid doom-filled opening line, *Call me Ishmael?* Let's see…

Moby Dick
Chapter 1
Frankly, I don't quite know how to introduce myself. I thought of using my real name, but somehow Herman didn't sound right, and neither did Sam or Harold or any of a hundred other names I thought of and discarded. Then one day — it was the darndest coincidence — I was strolling down Broad Street when I happened to bump into a friend I hadn't seen for years, and he had this really weird name, I mean, wacko! And so……

I can't decide whether the computer is helping to create better literature or just more of it. The jury is still out.

჻

"Well, if you want to go back to prehistoric times, like B.C. —" my daughter said, when we were discussing this the other day. She had dropped in to borrow my vacuum cleaner. She recently bought the absolutely state-of-the-art computer setup. Now she can multi-task while she's downloading, she tells me, and I said Hotsy totsy! and she lifted an eyebrow. But she doesn't seem to mind her Smithsonian-type vacuum cleaner at all.

"Not *that* far back," I said. "They didn't even have decent pencils then."

"I mean Before Computers, Mama," my daughter said. She is always patient with me. "If you zapped the microchip you'd be zapping the dishwasher and the...."

"Goodness, no!" I said. I remembered when she was a little girl and we didn't have a dishwasher and I'd wash and she'd wipe, and that was a good time to talk. But I also remembered how I wished sometimes I could just sit down and read a book. Togetherness (as they used to call it) is okay, but not when your feet hurt, as they sometimes do when you're coping with a job and a house and a husband and a family. Life is simpler now, but you can't take my dishwasher.

"And that fancy washing-machine-dryer combo of yours that does everything but fold the clothes?" she continued gently. "That's all thanks to a microprocessor, you know. And all those bells and whistles in your car — you know, the window controls and your fuel injection system and all that? And the Home Security System that keeps you from being raped and slaughtered in your bed?" She does have a way of putting things.

"I — er — I'd better, uh, go call Howie about coming next week," I said, and left.

So I called Howie, but his answering machine said he'd split the scene and gone out to groove on some new action. Then I called and called my friend Rene about lunch the next day, but her cat must have knocked the phone off the table again. Then I called my friend Josephine, but we were interrupted after about six words — she has Call Waiting — so I slammed the phone down (temper, temper!) and took a bath, still pondering our alleged progress over the decades, and recalling the old days before Call Waiting and Call Forwarding, etc., etc., etc.

For one thing, I can't answer the telephone anymore at the dinner hour, because that is Telemarketer Time, when they crawl out of their holes to sell you something you can get along without very nicely, like tickets to the big golf tournament, the Tobacco Syndicate Open for the Benefit of the Lung-Disadvantaged. Does this further communication, to be afraid to answer your own phone?

ॐ

I had some good statistics at hand here, but luckily I lost them. As I remember, they concerned how many telephones have been lobbed out of how many windows, at consid-erable damage to panes and potted plants, by people who had finally had it with Press One, Press Two, Press Three, then a

Backward, turn backward,
O time in thy flight!
Un-invent telephones
Just for tonight!

recorded Please Hold, then four minutes of hot rock, then Please Hold, your business is important to us, your call will be answered as soon as one of our super-service representatives is available.

And Long Distance — the times you're calling from a pay phone, and AT&T won't take your Sprint card or vice-versa, and the taxi meter is ticking away. But we'd best not go into that.

It was only a few days later that my daughter stopped by again with her daughter, my granddaughter, who is fifteen, now, so she can't talk right; she's all "Hi, Granny-babes!" and I'm like, "Hello, Honey, why are you wearing a size 56 sweatshirt?"

I happened to mention the telephone situation and how efficient telephones used to be. You'd pick up the receiver and hear a pleasant "Number, please?" (That was known as the Voice with a Smile.) Then you'd ask for the Long Distance Operator, and there you'd be.

"Maybe so," my daughter said, "but she sure couldn't connect you with Nome, Alaska, or Three Sheep, New Zealand."

"Who wants to connect with Three Sheep, New Zealand?" I said, with some asperity.

"Mother, stop harking back," my daughter said. She has mentioned before that I seem to hark oftener these days. "So what about 911? And all those dandy little 800 numbers?"

I had to admit she had a couple of good points there. That's always the trouble, you see — there's a plus and a minus side to practically everything, as I believe I mentioned a good while ago.

"And what about the 900 numbers?" my grand-daughter said. A fact of life she learned the hard way is that 900 numbers cost money, and she restrains herself now. With difficulty. "And the Net," she added, "and the Web."

"I don't know anything about that," I said. "But did I ever tell you about the time — we'd just gotten engaged — and I was trying to locate your grandpa — we were at the beach — and I called Central — that's what you called the Operator then, and —"

"Yes, Mother, I think you did," my daughter said patiently.

"MEGO," my granddaughter said. She says that with frequency. It was a good while before I learned that MEGO means My Eyes Glaze Over.

"All the same," I said firmly. I don't know what all-the-same means, either, but I seem to say it quite a lot.

It was just about then that Howie and his boombox strolled past and we had to stop talking anyway. My granddaughter invited him in, and I thought we should mellow out a little and so I made us each a root beer float. It is nice that there are still things the generations are in total agreement about, and a root beer float is one of them.

ॐ

Let's see. My daughter will be my age in 2030. And what will she look fondly back to? Those quaint old-fashioned fast-food joints? Those evenings at home with the family gathered around a roaring TV set?

And my granddaughter will be my age in, say, 2060. Will she look back to the picturesque old days when she and her husband and the kids spent the evenings each with his own PC with a screen the size of the wall, surfing the Worldwide Web and the Net? But the way things are moving, all that will be totally obsolete by then.

Who can tell? But you can be sure there will be material. No generation has a corner on nostalgia.

ᔧ

In Retrospect

In retrospect the folk were kind,
and dreams and jokes and love were new,
and baby ducklings swam the pond,
and skies were blue as blue.

And dawns! As fresh as new-baked bread,
and pears were honey in the mouth,
and sunsets were the reddest red,
and winds were from the south.

So memory embroiders fact:
the air was bright, the trees were tall,
in retrospect, in Retrospect,
the fairest country of them all.

ॐ

And, as Franklin Pierce Adams put it, quite a few years ago, "Nothing is more responsible for the good old days than a bad memory."

Chapter Five

Etiquette and the Old Person

The younger person should not ask the Old person if he is still scuba-diving (windsurfing, playing tennis, driving, or whatever it is). Many younger citizens find it hard to believe that anyone over sixty-five can still totter from room to room unaided. If the Old person is still doing any or all of these things, he will probably mention it anyway, and the younger person should conceal his astonishment. Similarly, "Didn't you used to..." is often an unwise choice of words.

૱

Before the Old person accepts a dinner invitation, he should probably mention that he can't eat red meat or sour cream or whatever it is. Otherwise, he is apt to be faced with a heaping plateful of Beef Stroganoff and no lettuce leaf to hide it under, plus a hostess who wants to hit him with a hard roll.

૱

The young person should hide his dismay, should the Old person come out with something like, "Yowsa yowsa!" or start trucking. We all have a right to revert once in awhile.

✌

The Old person should take it calmly should a younger member of the family show up with a nose ring or a diamond-pierced lower lip or a Snoop Doggy Dog tattoo. Just an interested "Hmmm...very nice. Who does your body work?" is all that is required.

✌

Unless the Old person is positive he's talking to someone even older than he is, he should avoid the phrase "people our age."

✌

Waiters shouldn't ask two definitely ripe or Old customers, "And what'll you have, young ladies?" This happened the other day when I was lunching with a friend, who promptly gave him the single-digit salute. I deplored her manners but shared her sentiments.

ॐ

"Aren't you going to mention nose hair and ear hair?" my daughter asked. "You know, in old fellows?"

"I hadn't thought to," I said.

"Wouldn't that be etiquette too?" she said. "You know how some old guys get these absolute tufts of gray hair in their ears and noses, practically long enough to braid? I don't think it's very appetizing."

"Maybe not," I conceded, though I must admit that it never bothers me. After all, most of us Old persons keep losing hair all the time, and so when we get some extra, we're not about to quibble over where it lands. Hair is hair.

About ears, though, the silver-haired boss of a radio station where I once worked had a habit of inserting a little finger into an ear and excavating, with a remarkable digital vibrato. We kept wondering what he was delving for, and we wished he wouldn't do it, as we looked out the window, waiting for him to quit.

ॐ

Also, the young person mustn't assume that the Old person is entirely innocent of worldly matters, nor need he necessarily apologize for alluding to biological functions that were seldom mentioned a few decades ago except in the privacy of the Family Doctor's office, back when there was a Family Doctor. Now, we go to movies and watch television and read books and know where babies come from and everything. And unless the Old person has been living on an ice ledge at the top of Mount Kilimanjaro for the past six decades, she is most likely unshockable. I was reflecting the other day that nothing shocks me anymore. Or put it this way: Only the fact that nothing shocks me is what shocks me.[20]

‌⌣

Something I suppose we Old persons should beware of is a sort of hardening of the habits. This is the result of mental sludge that can settle in the brain, rather like the stuff Mr. Goodwrench pours out of your crankcase. There are things we inevitably say — a sort of Pavlovian reflex — should the trigger word be spoken. Like the wife in a *New Yorker* short story who always said "daffy-down-dillies" instead of daffodils, till her husband understandably left home for good.

And things we do. I've noticed that I have my favorite chair or sofa corner in any room where I often sit, and if it's occupied, I'm a trifle miffed. ("Get out of my chair!" she cackled, brandishing her cane.) Still, why not? I ask myself. Going downhill is uphill work.

---

20. A gentle white-haired Old friend of mine, however, became tired of hearing and seeing the F-word all over the place, and particularly of hearing herself mutter it when she'd upset the tomato juice pitcher in the refrigerator or perhaps discovered a run in her orthopedic stockings, or encountered some similar tiny disaster. So she substituted Fluff. "Oh, Fluff!" she says now when she is annoyed. To me this lacks a certain authoritative ring, but I admit it is a welcome change.

You might as well get as comfortable as you can wherever you can, I always say. And speaking of what I always say, there are anecdotes you're going to hear again from me, like it or not, should you mention Des Moines in my company. Or babies and how to name them. Or giraffes. It is a knee-jerk reflex with me. I don't know if there is a Twelve-Step Program that could help, but I'm going to find out.

ॐ

Something else: When the Old person leads off with, "When I was your age..." the younger person should not sigh deeply, roll his eyes, and gaze heavenward. Someday he may need an audience himself.[21]

On the other hand, as my daughter pointed out (daughters are good at pointing things out, like your pants are too short), the younger person gets a bit tired of trying to keep the Old person on track. For instance, she said, she'll be telling me about a friend's new boat, and I'll reply, "I wonder if that place in the mall still makes those good turkey sandwiches." I know this can be annoying, because only weeks ago I was telling a friend at some length about my cat's hip operation, and after I'd finished, she said, "By the way, how is that darling cat of yours?" My daughter also mentioned the 1000-yard Stare, which she says I do frequently. When I do, she knows I'm only halfway listening, because

---

21. "A healthy male adult bore consumes each year one-and-a-half times his own weight in other people's patience." –John Updike

I'm mostly deciding what I'm going to butt in with when she stops for breath.

And then there are the Space Invaders, she said, who edge closer and closer as they talk, so you can admire the spinach in their teeth. I agreed that we senior types probably do that more than the juniors do, but we have a better excuse. Sometimes it is because our hearing isn't quite what it used to be, and we'd like to know what you're talking about.

Which reminds me: my daughter and I were having a pre-dinner drink at the airport restaurant before she caught a plane the other evening. (She is aiming to break the glass ceiling, and she travels a lot, always with modem, cellular phone, and her faithful laptop computer.)

"Well, tell me," she said, "how's it going?"

"How's what going?" I said. "The book? Or getting old?"

"The book," she said.

"Like clockwork," I said. "Sometimes it goes, sometimes it stops."

"But now that you mention it, how's the getting old part?" she said.

"What?" I asked.

"Mom, you've been saying 'What?' quite a lot lately," she said gently. "Do you think maybe you should see an ear doctor?"

Oh dear, I thought to myself. *Something else now?* Only that morning I'd had a slight problem getting up off the floor. I was hunting for a book on the bottom shelf and couldn't quite coordinate my knees with the rest of me. I thought I'd have to stay on the floor till the swallows came back to wherever it is they come back to, and this wasn't the season.

"I think you're in denial," my daughter added. (Was there just a touch here of the condescension the young so often feel for the Old? Though no more, I suppose, than the Old so often feel for the young. I remember a cartoon that lived on my mother's refrigerator for years — the proud college graduate saying to the world, "See? I've got my A.B.!" and the world saying, "That's fine, sonny. Now I'll teach you the rest of the alphabet.")

In denial, she'd said. "Oh, I don't think so," I said airily, fishing the cherry out of my Manhattan while she sipped her designer mineral water. "Anyway, if I *am* getting deaf, I don't think I'm missing much."

"How can you tell unless you hear it?" she said. "Remember how mad you used to get at Grandma because she simply refused to admit she needed glasses that time she thought the soy sauce was vanilla and loused up the cake?"

"Anyone could do that," I said.

"Yeah, right," she said. "That isn't what you told Grandma."

I suppose I did let my irritation get the better of me once in awhile, in my mother's later years. She was stubborn, as only an Old lady can be. And cranky. Really cantankerous sometimes. I think too that the young are gifted with superb memories, when they want to use them, so they can remember things like this and make their elders feel stupid. It's the Law of

Compensation. After all, they spent the first quarter of *their* lives hearing, blow your nose, sit up straight, eat your nice parsnips. I suppose it's their turn now.

And so I left her at Gate 7 to go back to the fast track, feeling the twinge I always feel when she leaves — a shadow of the major twinge I felt on her first day of school as I watched her toddle off into the real world, all by herself.

ॐ

On the way home, I was thinking back to our conversation, and I found I was looking myself in the eye, which is hard to do when you're driving, and probably illegal as well, but I did it anyway. *Crabby. Maybe working up to cantankerous? Recently I'd certainly been sweating the little stuff, which all those bumper stickers and office placards tell you not to do.*

And then I thought, *Mom, I wish you were here so we could talk about this. I'm beginning to realize why you were, well, a little difficult. I think it's because when you're an Old person you begin to feel insecure. When you can't — CHECK ONE OR ALL — (hear) (see) (move) (remember) quite as well as you used to, you're at the mercy of the winds that blow. People can tell you it's Wednesday, not Tuesday, and you might as well believe them. They can say with disbelief, "You mean to tell me you don't remember the day we walked to the Falls and saw the blue heron?" But you don't, and so you feel vulnerable — What's this, the begin-*

nings of Oldtimer's Disease? Yipe! So maybe you lie a little. "Oh yes, of course!" you say. "Wasn't he beautiful!", meanwhile feeling as though your steering wheel has become somewhat detached from the rest of the car.

Mom, I'm sorry.

ॐ

And so, getting back to Etiquette, though we didn't get very far away from it, I thought maybe a good part of Old Person Etiquette is recognizing limitations and doing something about them if possible.

Like, don't accuse people of mumbling; get yourself a sound-system.

If you've been tangling lately with cops and cars, don't be too dogged about driving.

And don't pretend you're rugged enough for a strenuous outing when you know you're not, then poop the party midway with a "No, I insist! You all just go on and have a good time; I don't mind waiting here for three hours, *really!*"

ॐ

Opinion is split along gender lines on the next topic, *Ailments as Conversation,* though there is no arguing their popularity among Old persons in general. And no wonder! The slings and arrows of outrageous fortune turn nearly all Old persons into veterans of one battle or another, with battle scars and stitches to prove it. Take a group of Old persons, especially of the female persuasion, and you'll likely harvest — among other things, of course — a bumper crop of what Emerson called "distempers."

> *"There is one topic peremptorily forbidden to all well-bred, to all rational mortals, namely their distempers. If you have not slept, or if you have a headache, or sciatica, or leprosy, or thunderstroke, I beseech you, by all the angels, to hold your peace."*
>
> – *Ralph Waldo Emerson*

Spoken like a Concord philosopher with his head in the clouds! But much as I hate to disagree with a man I heartily admire, I believe he overstates his case here. Personally I can think of many conversational topics less appealing than distempers, and I speak from experience.

"So we took I-5 to Redding, then 299 to Eureka, and I think it was 101 to Willits, or no, maybe we cut off at Willits, or — Edith, did we cut off at Willits?"

"Lemme tell you about this terrific movie we saw last night on the tube. I forget the name of it, but there's this young fellow, see, and he wins a million bucks, only the lottery won't pay off, because..."

"...And so Ernie, he's my nephew in Altoona — no, you never met him — he gets this great job with Amalgamated Gear, mainly hypoids and helicals? But then the company tunes up for pawls, you know, for one-directional rotation...?"

No thanks, Mr. Emerson, I'll take leprosy anytime. Or thunderstroke! How exciting! Where were you when it hit? Did you see the lightning first or hear the thunder? What did it feel like? Did it hurt?

Indeed, ailments have gotten a bad rap as conversational fodder, and I think it is mainly because of men, who fell right into lockstep with Emerson. Just notice, next time you're in a doctor's waiting room. Women will be happily comparing operations, with full details,[22] while men shift uneasily on those turquoise Naugahyde sofas and leaf through a last year's *Reader's Digest.*

Which is only logical. After all, there were women before there were doctors. Back in the cave days, every woman was a midwife if the situation demanded, while the man-of-the-cave was out hunting another saber-toothed tiger, and if the tiger won that round, it was probably women who found the herbs and applied the poultices. We are more naturally interested in things medical, and men are strangely dainty when it comes to cleaning up messes.

Don't we need a magic pill
or potion that protects
A person from the side effects
of all the side effects?

---

22. According to the southern writer Florence King, southern women spend considerable time comparing how far their wombs have dropped. It seems to be rather a contest, though I doubt that the event will ever make the Olympics.

It is true — and most women would agree — that Aunt Carrie could shut up for awhile about her sinuses, but then she's a Career Invalid anyway. Sore feet can be rather a bore too. But if you've had a really wicked operation or you're turning green all over and three specialists can't figure out why, we'd love to hear about it.

৵

Which brings us naturally to some sticky wickets which the Old person will be maneuvering around presently if not now. She is apt to be sending more Get Well cards and writing more notes and learning the best parking spots around the various hospitals, if she doesn't know them already.

About Get Well cards, the consensus is that they're fine if they're funny and the patient is only moderately sick — say, a three on a scale of ten. Norman Cousins, being a staunch believer in the curative powers of humor, watched a good many old Marx Brothers movies in his hospital room and said they helped a great deal. He knew that laughter releases a flock of endorphins — those pain-relieving proteins we store in our brains — right into the bloodstream. No wonder a laugh a day is supposed to keep the doctor away. Or is it an apple? No matter, a laugh is probably better, though the sound of all that jollity in Room No. 203 might well bring the doctor right in. Most doctors can use a good laugh too.

But if the patient is seriously sick, pulling a nine on that same one-to-ten scale, he probably knows it, with a sort of basic body knowledge. Any one of those super-cheerful cards — *(You'll Soon Be Right as Rain, I Know — a Little Bluebird Told Me So!!)* could make him even sicker, especially when his chances of leaving that hospital bed alive are minimal. Better to send a short affectionate note: "We're pulling for you and we send our love" — perhaps tucked into a bunch of daisies or a teddy bear's paw. No one is too old for a teddy bear.

Then, telephone calls. My own feeling is that they should be brief and not too frequent. I once had a friend who called and *called,* so solicitous you'd have thought she was going to inherit. This didn't cheer me up. I thought, *What does she know about my interesting condition that I don't?*

And visits. Most important here is to find out if the patient wants any. If he does, keep it short. But many people hate to be seen at their horizontal worst, and visitors are a strain, no matter what. When I'm the patient and visitors come, I always feel like the hostess with the leastest, fluffing up again. And with visitors you have to act brave — *She's such a good sport!* — when maybe you'd rather just lie there and whimper, all by yourself.

᠀

It was right here that my Word Processor lost two whole pages of this Chapter Five and tried to blame it on me. It flashed a message when I tried to retrieve them — YOU LACK SUFFICIENT MEMORY TO ACCESS CHAP. 5 — or something of the sort, and my first thought was, *This is news?* And my second thought was, *Mind your manners.*

What it meant, though, was that *it* lacked sufficient memory, as I learned when I called Barbara my Computer Guru, who straightens me out when things look black. She said I must buy more memory for this machine. Then I won't have any more problems. Of that sort, anyway, she amended prudently. But even she couldn't find the missing two pages, and the computer hasn't coughed them up yet.

I didn't know then how you buy memory — by the pound or the yard or the quart? — but I was wishing I could buy some for myself too. I'd take all they've got, short term and long term both. Wait a minute. On second thought, I'd as soon skip age sixteen through twenty-three, but I'd like a big helping of twenty-four and up.

As for short term, the geriatrics experts aren't just whistling *Auld Lang Syne* when they say it gets bad fast.[23] Like, I couldn't tell you at the count of five, or even ten, what I had for lunch yesterday. Or the name

---

23. This isn't to say that people don't forget things when they are younger, even teens and baby boomers. But with them, as they will be happy to explain, it's because they are preoccupied with other and major things — the teens with growing up, which demands constant attention, and the BBs with being Masters of the Universe.

of the pessimistic tax man I met last night. Or where I put my glasses.

For that's another problem: mislaying things. No wonder it takes the Old person a bit longer, getting ready to go to the movies. She must change handbags, because the brown one looks terrible with her black shoes. So she hunts for the black one, to the accompaniment of vigorous honking from whoever she's going with. But when she finally finds the black purse, she remembers she left her billfold in the brown one, but where did she put the brown one? She had it just a MINUTE ago!! It was RIGHT HERE! (But the delay isn't all bad. They'll miss the Previews of Coming Attractions.)

༄

Now that I think of it, there is an associated etiquette point that belongs here, and I think I'll include it, in place of the part the computer swallowed. When something is mislaid, the Old person has permission to sock the person who says, "But where did you have it last?" *(Dolt! Moron! If I knew that, I'd know where it is.)* And if that other person says, "Honestly, you'd lose your head if it wasn't fastened on," the Old person can hit him again.

༄

There remain a few items in the Etiquette department that should be mentioned, but I can't find my
notes. Perhaps they are in the brown handbag. So I will
wait until it finds me before I proceed, and then I'll put
them in the next chapter.

Chapter Six

~~Never~~ Always Say Die

Far from viewing it with awe,
I find the thought beguiling.
After all, you never saw
A skull that wasn't smiling.

At a banquet last night, the guest speaker began by telling us that "No generality is worth a damn, including this one." That was probably the best thing he said, but the strawberry mousse was delivered about then, and I missed a lot. Waiters should wait, sometimes, longer than they do.

But this morning, beginning this chapter, I thought that his remark was certainly true of Robert Browning's cheery first lines of Rabbi Ben Ezra...

"Grow old along with me!
The best is yet to be,
The last of life, for which the first was made."

His own life would testify to the truth of it. His early days were so-so, till he met and fell in love with Elizabeth Barrett, and then it became glorious. Even after she died, it wasn't all that bad, as his poetry began to outshine hers in public esteem, and you know how men are.

But not everyone feels the same about getting Old, and especially about death and dying. Indeed, we have not even agreed upon our terms for it, and a great many of us find the very words hard to say out loud.

While we have only recently become Politically Correct in many areas — the Indian is now called the Native American, and the fellow who waters the greenhouse greenery is now a Horticultural Technician, we have *always* been Politically Correct about death and dying, even in impolite discourse, which substitutes "kick the bucket," "buy the farm," "go west," "crap out" and a hundred other terms, usually spoken with a certain embarrassed jocularity, to avoid the dreadful word "die."

As for polite society, the words are fuzzier still, and unfortunately they strike an impudent chord in the mind of the irreverent listener. "We lost him." *(How careless of you.)* "He left us." *(How much?)* "He is no longer with us." *(Finally fired, was he?)* "Gone to meet his Maker." *(Another GM recall?)* All these are reminiscent of the British music hall dialogue, "Yesterday we buried Grandmother," and the solicitous response, "She was dead, I trust?"

Meanwhile, back at the mortuary, they're talking cremains[24] and slumber rooms.

What is the matter with the word "die"? I rise to its defense. It is a pretty word, soft as a sigh — rhymes with it, too, always handy for the versifier. And it says what it means, which is a real plus.

But to be fair, perhaps the word or words you choose depend a lot on what you think will happen after you do it. Die, I mean. Whether you expect to be

---

24. Is "cremains" really a better word than "ashes"? "Cremains to cremains, dust to dust" just doesn't cut it.

reincarnated, or reinvented (a popular procedure these days) or recycled like the plastic milk jug I emptied this morning, or heading for some marvelous land, luminous beyond imagining, your choice here must make a difference in how you phrase it. (One other popular euphemism should be mentioned: "If anything should happen to me." Note the word "anything." That means death. Note also the word "if." Here, the realist wants to say, "Face facts, fella. It isn't If, it's When.")

We all know this, of course. Yet it isn't a general topic of conversation even among us Old persons. Though we are drawing closer and closer to what Henry James called "the Distinguished Thing," we seldom talk or speculate about it together, except possibly in church, and not often then.

This seems odd to me, because it has been such an intriguing mystery through the ages. The people we know who — dare I say it? — died are not communicating. They never phone, never write, never fax. Emerson said, as he was dying, "The reality is more excellent than the report." But how did he know? He was only dying, not dead. And then there is the near-death experience one hears so much about. But neither is that a *fait accompli.*

It is as though we are all on a big bus, not many of us being totally sure of its destination. (The others, who are very sure indeed, tend to be sensitive, and they will fight at the drop of a hat if you disagree.) The bus driver won't tell us where we're going, either, though he keeps dropping tantalizing hints that we interpret in various ways.

Are we heading for Pittsburgh? Paris? Paducah? Or, to put it another way, will our bus driver pull over and park by the legendary Pearly Gates? Or in the Happy Hunting Ground Parking Lot & Gambling Casino, Admission Free? Or will he let us out at Valhalla or Paradise or Elysium or Nirvana? (I feel sorry for people who believe in a literal Hades and think that's where they're going. It must make dying harder than it needs to be. Still, if that's where they think they are headed, they probably deserve it. Looking at the bright side, they'll probably meet some interesting people there.)

Or are we simply going for the long, long sleep, safe, snug, and unconscious, the way we were for all the millennia before we arrived here? That is an appealing prospect too.

> *"The sensation of falling asleep is to me the most delightful in the world. I relish it so much that I even look forward to death itself with a sneaking wonder and desire."*
> – H.L. Mencken

And I remember reading about some old French nobleman who so loved the process of going to sleep that he had his servant wake him up four or five times a night.

As I said, it is a grand mystery and a fascinating topic to ruminate on and to speculate about. And yet we hardly ever do it aloud! As the bus goes rollicking along, we go right ahead talking about the weather, the stock market, the kids, the grandkids, what's the best pizza place in town, or about the most recent terrorist action that put a good many people on a fast bus that left a few days ago.

Of course, there are good reasons we don't want to talk about death. One is that talking about it brings it right into the parlor — makes it even more of a reality, if that is possible. And we like living. There is simply a natural reluctance to leave a good party — if it *is* a good party — for parts unknown, so let's not think about it. And there is a certain wistfulness. *I love this little planet, and why do I have to leave it? Why does it have to leave me? What will it do without me? And what will I do without it?* A feeling of lostness can set in, and it helps only a little to think of the thousands of millennia we did without each other and did just fine, thanks.

And there is something else. Contrary to the classical picture of the Old person — Patience in a rocking chair — many of us find it a more intensely alive time than any we've known before. The fizz has not gone out of the champagne. You realize profoundly that there aren't that many sunrises and sunsets left — not that many days to look at and love a begonia or a friend or a spouse or a child or a cat or a tune or a picture or a — well, anything at all! And you realize what a microscopic peephole you've been looking through all your life, in a world so full of riches that it would take how many lifetimes to encompass them. *(Hey, maybe there's something to reincarnation after all! Maybe we'll get some more chances! But wait a minute, next time around maybe you'd be a — let's see*

— an aardvark? And I'd be a — well, a petunia? Do you suppose you get to choose? A friend of mine wants to be a rogue elephant. Will they let her? I must look into this.)

Speaking for myself, I have always had the sense of something "overarching and undergirding the universe that men have always called God," in Dr. Waldemar Argow's good words. But what happens after this fleeting segment of consciousness, or where the bus is going, I just don't know. My own feeling is, **Surprise me!**

In any case, you might feel that it is too soon to die. Life being a continuous cliffhanger, you want to see at least some of what happened after you left. Who got elected? Did they get the new library built?

If I should die before I wake
I pray the Lord my soul to take,
Though I, myself, can't go before
I've straightened out my
underwear drawer.

Did they find any men on Mars or women on Venus? Did your grandson shape up? Or maybe it will all seem so trivial you'll wonder why you ever gave it a thought. Or maybe there is no part of you left to wonder.

Or perhaps there is a project you always meant to finish, or someone you need to take care of, or a goal you promised yourself you'd reach.

And another thing — do you have your Last Words figured out? If you make your final exit in the Intensive Care Unit, you'll not be able to say them, and so it is a good thing to write them down — a summation, a comment, or anything that will sound good and look nice. If it's brief enough, it can mark your tombstone too, or the jar containing your ashes — oops! — cremains.

George Bernard Shaw's last words were, "Well, it will be a new experience, anyway." My Uncle Matt's were, fittingly enough, "I'm about to join the majority." (Uncle Matt had always been politically inclined but a minority voter. True enough, there are a great many more dead people in the world than any other kind.) A friend of mine, clearly a man of few words, wanted the words "I tried."

But when I think of all the good Last Words I have heard, I like best Doris Medina's:[25] "Will you please turn off the television?"

⍝

Back to the original premise: too soon! Some people think, for whatever reason and whenever it is, not *yet.* As a friend's mother put it plaintively just before she died, "Dammit, just when I was getting the hang of it!" And then, some people are afraid they won't do it right. An old school friend of mine was told

---

25. Mother of John J. Medina, author of *The Clock of Ages* (Cambridge University Press, 1996.)

by her doctor that it would probably be in a few weeks, and she was nervous about it. "I hope I don't miss my cue," she said to me. I could have reassured her with Montaigne's words on the subject, had I known them then:

> *"If you know not how to die, never trouble yourself. Nature will in a moment fully and sufficiently instruct you; she will exactly do that business for you, take no care for it."*

_ɔ_

And yet the other side of the coin presents the bigger problem: Those who want to die right now but can't, because society won't let them.

Antique maps inscribe an uncharted and fearsome part of the ocean:

There Be Dragons

and indeed there be. I suppose we'll always have some. But today's are a different kind. They are usually disguised as white-coated scientists and well-meaning doctors who feel it is their duty to keep despairing patients stuck full of high-tech equipment to keep them existing, not living, in their private pain-wracked hell or in their vegetable world.

Which takes us back to Brother Ass, whom we met in Chapter 2. He has not turned against you, but he is mortally tired. Think how many niggling infirmities he has licked for you, not to mention some possibly big ones. Now he is simply succumbing to the dying that is built into his system.[26] There can come a time when the "annoying impertinences of aging" (to quote Gus Arriola) grow into something bigger, as Brother Ass's various parts wear out. Presently the Old person may find himself the center of a whole spiderweb of complications — the heart trouble leading to the lung trouble, the throat trouble leading to the stomach trouble, the hip bone connected to the thigh bone, the thigh bone connected to the — you know the drill. And you don't know precisely what you're suffering from, but nothing seems to be working at all well, and you feel like a couple hundred miles of bad road.

This is the time to thank yourself for being farsighted enough, back when you were healthy, to make some legal preparations, sign all the proper papers, and make sure you tell your doctor what eventual indignities you'll put up with and which ones you won't. *And,* if you possibly can, avert a panicked trip to the hospital. For that is where high-tech and impersonal medicine would guarantee your living long enough to make it to Twilight Acres, a nifty suburban nursing home that's only $5000 a month, where you'll survive forever as just one more problem in personal plumbing.[27]

---

26. "Death keeps taking little bits of me," said an old lady quoted by Dr. Nuland in *How We Die,* Knopf, 1995.

27. A sensible old Roman named Attilus, in the third century B.C., said, "Not only a prudent, brave, or wretched man may wish to die, but even a fastidious one."

I have always liked the old Irish blessing: "God give you a long life and a short death."

~

A Unitarian minister whose name I do not know has, with no sacrilegious intent, painted the whole picture in his *Psalm for Today:*

Medical Science is my shepherd;
I shall not want,
It maketh me to lie down in hospital beds;
It leadeth me beside the marvels of technology.
It restoreth my brain waves;
It maintains me in a persistent vegetative state
  for its name's sake.
Yea, though I walk through the valley of the
  shadow of death,
I will find no end to life;
Thy respirator and heart machine they sustain me.
Thou preparest intravenous feeding for me
In the presence of irreversible disability;
Thou annointest my head with oil;
My cup runneth on and on and on and on.
Surely coma and unconsciousness shall follow me
  all the days of my continued breathing;
And I will dwell in the intensive care unit forever.

~

And so we run into the good old cliché, *If we can put a man on the moon, why can't we figure out a humane and decent way for us to die when we are ready?* It is true, good people are working on it now, while unenlightened people are building roadblocks. And meanwhile, whatever happened to hemlock?

ᘐ

We come now to the matter of condolence messages. I am sending more of them these days, because — like most Old persons — I know more people on the Obit page than I used to. It is too bad that an awkward native shyness often prevents our expressing the emotion we feel, and so we let an impersonal card carry our personal sentiments. Just a simple "I was very fond of Larry, and he has left a large empty hole in my life" is often better than a handsome card replete with poetic sentiments.

And sometimes the wrong sentiment is chosen. A man I know whose wife died recently received a pretty, lily-strewn sympathy card that said, "She isn't gone, she is just away." Inasmuch as he was already seeing another lady, it came as rather a jolt.

Another point about the far end of the trail: There seem to be more personal death announcements being sent these days by the family of the one who died.[28] Perhaps it seems that way only because my contempo-

---

28. I just can't bring myself to say "the deceased."

raries and I are now at that age. In fact, I received a typewritten one not long ago from a dead friend herself — a rather jolly note it was — saying, "I just thought you'd like to know I died last Thursday" (you can believe I scrutinized the postmark carefully at that point) — "and I know I'm going to miss you and all the fun we had together." I finally came to the reluctant conclusion that she had dictated and left it with her family for them to fill in the blanks and mail.

It is a thoughtful thing to do, I think — I mean sending an announcement of some kind — because you never know the size of the space you occupy in other people's lives. It might be called "existence value" — a term used by insurance people for those items that have little monetary value, necessarily, but would leave a big empty space in your life if they were to disappear. It might be an accordion you're going to learn some day, or an old boat you love but never use now. Nevertheless, the knowledge that it is *there* is a warming thought in your mind, rather like Garrison Keillor's storm home.

He tells somewhere about the storm homes his third-grade class were assigned as a precautionary measure against the cruel Minnesota winters. Each child had a friendly nearby house to go to, should the weather turn unexpectedly worse and he couldn't make it home from school. As it turned out, he never got to use it. But always it was a sustaining thought. He knew it was *there*.

I think this applies to people too. Just the knowledge that you're somewhere on the planet may be a storm home for certain people, whether you see them or hear from them frequently or not. Therefore, it seems to me a good thing for you or the family to let them know that the storm home is closed, at least for the season. Not everyone reads the Obits or lives in the same town.

    It could be simple — indeed, the simpler the better:
Dear _____ ,

    I'm sure Pete would want you to know that he died on Tuesday, July 23. A memorial service will be announced later.

    His friendship with you meant a lot to Pete, and I do thank you for being such a good part of his life.

    Sincerely,

_____

    Or it could be a little more detailed —
Dear _____ ,

    Your good friend and my dear wife Polly died at home on Monday, December 9. She had been ill for several weeks with pneumonia, and a memorial service will be held at

_____

on December 9 at 2 o'clock.

    Her family and I are so sorry to give you this news, but I know you will think of her as fondly as I know she thought of you.

    Sincerely,

_____

And, if you like, you could include a favorite motto or verse of the one who died.

I am preparing my own announcement right now, to make sure my family spells my name right; also to see that some lovely words of Thoreau's are included:

"So we saunter toward the Holy Land, till one day the sun shall shine more brightly than ever he has done, shall perchance shine into our minds and hearts, and light up our whole lives with a great awakening light, as warm and serene and golden as a bank-side in autumn."

Chapter Seven

Great Truths and
Small Wonders

Old and Wise
The two go hand in hand,
It's said, but still I worry.
The *old* arrived as planned,
But I wish the *wise* would hurry!

After living for a fair number of years, one should have learned a few things — harvested at least a small crop of pertinent insights to impart to other people, if only they'd hold still.

Aldous Huxley felt this way but was disappointed in what he was able to come up with. In his later years he wrote that "it is a bit embarrassing to have been concerned with the human problem all one's life and find at the end that one has no more to offer by way of advice than, *'Try to be a little kinder.'*"

Admittedly, this isn't as worldshaking as one might expect. And yet it is hard to think of anything more fundamental. I certainly couldn't, when I was trying to rake together my own gleanings which, in all humility, I offer here.

1. It often helps to read the directions.

2. *Accommodate* is spelled with two Cs and two Ms.

3. You can do everything right and it can still turn out wrong.

4. The most unlikely-looking people were once cute babies.

5. You don't always get what you pay for. Sometimes more, sometimes less.

6. Handsome or famous
        or stupid or clever,
    the friends that you laugh with
        you cherish forever.

7. Everything takes longer than you think it should, except for some things that don't take as long.

8. If kittens and dandelions weren't free, they would get more respect.

9. Most people feel guiltier about eating the double chocolate mousse than they do about not paying for it, if the waiter neglects to put it on the check.

10. The three-minute soft-boiled egg must have meant straight from the hen. Straight from the fridge, it looks like a cold in the head. Six minutes is fine.

11. Intolerance is okay depending on what you're intolerant of. Like, you can be intolerant of intolerance.

12. Almost all trouble starts out like fun. It was fun eating all those doughnuts, but now you can't get into your jeans.

13. Between sixty and eighty-five there is as much difference as between fifteen and forty.

14. *"...in this Mortal state of imperfection Fig leaves are as necessary for our Minds as our Bodies, and 'tis as indecent to show all we think as what we have."*
    – Lady Mary Wortley Montagu

15. On their return from a trip, it is wise to see friends promptly, before they've had time to get their pictures developed.

16. Hard brown sugar will soften if you put a cupful in a microwave bowl with a slice of bread and zap it on high for thirty to sixty seconds.

17. Every solution breeds another problem. Now you will have to hurry and bake something with it before it gets hard again.

ॐ

The Cockroach Killer

We must love the living, we know, or perish,
for hate means nukes, which affect the breathing
adversely. Still, can't we choose and cherish
one object of hate or — let's say, loathing?
To quit cold turkey would shock the system,
for most of us have too many to list 'em.

So I, after no indecision, chose roaches.
You can have flies, or worms, or snakes,
or spiders, or slippery slugs, or leeches,
but roaches are mine — Mother Nature's
*   mistakes,*
I've always felt — and wherever I've found them,
I'd take my shoe and earnestly pound them,
but still, like as not, they'd scuttle away.
(Oh, the Roach will inherit the earth, they say.)

Well, early today, at five in the a.m.
I found myself suddenly ready for mayhem
and murder, as suddenly there — right there! —
came the Cockroach King, from under a chair!
He didn't see me, but I saw him,
and I stomped and scattered him, limb from limb,
and fixed him good, though I must add
*   that this had nothing to do with good,*
*   but all to do with Original Sin.*

And suddenly I was scared. The blood
roared loud in my ears, as I
*   understood*
in a flash why the world's in the
*   shape it's in:*
*   precisely because I could get so*
*   mad.*

But, of course, there are great numbers of things
one can't be too sure of. As the seasons turn, replacing
each other with remarkable speed, the Old person is
apt to find herself more often in the position —
generally a sitting-down position — of having time to
think but not all that much to think about. Or, to be
quite personal for a moment, I do. My feet are up and
my mind is in neutral.

There I am, waiting in the car to pick somebody up, or for someone to come back to it. Or sitting in a waiting room — doctor's, dentist's, lawyer's, whichever it is, he's "running behind," as his receptionist puts it with a cheery smile. I don't especially want to think about the approaching pelvic exam or root canal or codicil revision and what it's going to cost me. That's when I frequently find myself wondering about things.

ॐ

I wonder...

1. why they say "growing up," when actually you grow down. By the time you're an Old person, the cartilage between your discs has probably become a bit mashed, like sofa cushions, but you can't plump it up. Therefore, you may end up an inch or two shorter, though certainly not as short as you started out.

2. where pounds go when you lose them. With so many people dieting, there ought to be hundreds of pounds floating around out there, but I've never bumped into any.

3. if the guillotine hurt. The man who invented it said it didn't — said people felt only a slight chill. Some doctors doubted that.

4. why they don't ever put toothpaste in pretty tubes that will match the towels.

5. why the Miscellaneous folder in my expanding file is the only one that ever expands.

6. why that lady buried her lover's head in a pot of basil, in that poem by Keats. Why would anyone do a thing like that?

7. is the world sort of falling apart, or do I think so because I am?

8. if I will ever learn to fold a roadmap instead of wadding it up.

9. why I am vaguely disappointed in an airport when the person they are paging isn't me (even though I know the message is probably some sparkler like "Uncle Ernie can't meet you; call a cab.").

10. why cats always wash their paws after they eat. Of course they would want to, after eating a messy mouse, but their paws don't get messy just eating catfood out of a bowl.

11. why I didn't figure that out sooner. (They're not washing their paws; they are washing their faces, Stupid.)

12. if cat doors give cats a headache.

13. why "invaluable" means valuable, instead of not valuable. After all, "indecent" means not decent and "independent" means not dependent and "insolent" means...er...not solent.

14. if I will ever know port from starboard without doing a double-think.

15. if I will ever learn to measure twice and cut once, instead of the other way around.

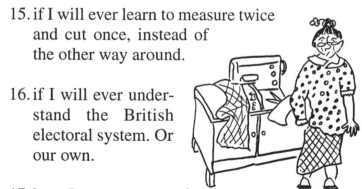

16. if I will ever understand the British electoral system. Or our own.

17. how I ever got out of the sixth grade.

18. why we don't celebrate the world's birthday. It isn't as though we don't know when it

was. The Archbishop of Armagh said, in 1620, that the world was created on the 22nd of October, 4004 B.C., at six o'clock in the evening. Why don't we celebrate it with plenty of cake and champagne and noise-makers and funny hats?

October 22 (Libra)

World, you are courageous, ambitious, and apprehensive of just about everything, and with good reason. Being very impressionable, you readily react to your environment. It is accordingly necessary to choose the right sort of companions and inhabitants. Hang in there!

ॐ

Postscript:

And so I handed the finished manuscript to the editor and told him that I'd been thinking, writing a book is rather like growing a tree. You start with a seed or a cutting, which you water faithfully and treat kindly, and with luck it will grow into a tree. Or a book.

Then you manicure it as best you can, trimming an awkward branch here and there, and cutting off any unsightly growths that happen to be left.

But because you are so close to it, you generally don't catch them all. And I warned him that if some unsightly growths were still in the manuscript, it wasn't my fault, it was the computer's. As I have pointed out, it hides things, but usually not forever, and they can pop up exactly when you don't want them.

"Hmmmmm," the editor said.

So home again, this voyage past,
All travelers' checks and passion spent.
So home again, to learn at last,
Familiarity breeds content.

About the Author

P eg Bracken has written a lot (nine books, much verse, syndicated columns), read a lot (everything in sight including aspirin labels), traveled a lot (here and mostly there), made many speeches (some dull, some okay, she says), and thought a bit, since the publication of *The I Hate to Cook Book,* when millions of women found her to be a kindred spirit and a good companion.

She is married to John Ohman, former Deputy Chief for Research of the U.S. Forest Service, and they live — naturally enough — where there are a great many trees, in Portland, Oregon. They find it a good place to get old for the first time, and so does their durable Siamese cat.